# RUBÁIYÁT OF OMAR KHAYYÁM

# Rubáiyát of
# OMAR KHAYYÁM

*Rendered into English verse by*
## EDWARD FITZGERALD

*Edited by*
## GEORGE F. MAINE

*Illustrated by*
## ROBERT STEWART
## SHERRIFFS

## COLLINS
## GLASGOW AND LONDON

NEW EDITION 1947
LATEST REVISED EDITION 1954
LATEST REPRINT 1982

The publishers wish to express their thanks to Cambridge University
Library, Professor J. Arberry Litt.D., F.B.A. and Messrs. John Murray
(Publishers) Ltd. for permission to include in the essay on Edward
FitzGerald in this volume, three quatrains from the "Teheran"
manuscript. This, the earliest known version of the *Rubáiyát*, was
acquired by Cambridge University Library in 1950, translated by
Professor Arberry, and published by Messrs. Murray in 1952.

ISBN 0 00 410551 6
ISBN 0 00 410553 2 (Luxury Edition)

PRINTED IN GREAT BRITAIN

COLLINS CLEAR-TYPE PRESS: LONDON AND GLASGOW

# CONTENTS

# ILLUSTRATIONS

The twelve illustrations in this edition are printed in four colours by the offset process.

# INTRODUCTION

FOR the great bulk of English readers – if in this connection a "great bulk" of readers can be predicated – the *Rubáiyát* of Omar Khayyám means the one particular translation done so divinely well by Edward FitzGerald, when the Victorian era was at its most self-centred and self-sufficient stage of development.

The poem made so little mark on its first appearance – so little mark with the critics and the general public, that is to say – that the original edition, passing out of sight, became presently a delightful rarity for the next generation of second-hand book lovers to unearth, for the high appreciation in two kinds which was then awaiting it – the literary and the monetary. And it remains essentially, like all other translations – even the authorised version of the Bible – a second-hand book.

For the translator of poetry and vision always stands between us and the original. And whatever the beauty, or the exact meaning of the original may have been, in this case we can hardly doubt that, for English minds, the translator has given to it a reconciling beauty and flavour of his own, which make it more acceptable to all but scholars or pedants.

Of this, indeed, we have proof in the very free and pliant variants of the rival versions – the earlier and the later – which are so fortunately available; and it is only necessary to compare FitzGerald's amended form of the opening stanza with his original, to realise how large a liberty he gave himself when rendering into English the richly-coloured similes of the East.

> " Wake! For the Sun behind yon Eastern height
> Has chased the Session of the Stars from Night;
> And, to the field of Heav'n ascending, strikes
> The Sultán's Turret with a Shaft of Light."

7

That is one version; this is the other, and the earlier:-

> " Awake! for Morning in the Bowl of Night
> Has flung the Stone that puts the Stars to Flight:
> And Lo! the Hunter of the East has caught
> The Sultán's Turret in a Noose of Light."

Both are charming – many, I think, would hold that the earlier is the better; but the existence of variants so widely different informs us definitely that FitzGerald's rendering is an inspired paraphrase rather than a translation. What he began doing – westernising, the better to acclimatise, his importation from Persia in the eleventh to England in the nineteenth century – he went on doing with added touches and second thoughts throughout his elaboration of the whole poem: the strange similes, in the earlier version of the stanza just quoted, are softened and made more graceful in the amended one. And still more strikingly is this shown in the first line of the stanza which follows, where the fantastic imagery of the earlier version –

> " Dreaming, when Dawn's Left Hand was in the sky " –

becomes changed to the more graceful but more ordinary –

> " Before the phantom of False Morning died."

Probably, in the present day, we could have stood, and even welcomed, a good deal more of the bizarrerie of Eastern fancy, under the smooth and almost perfect diction of FitzGerald's presentation of it, than he allowed to remain in his more finished version. But FitzGerald, though a recluse in his day, was still a Victorian – of an unusual kind; and it was in a Victorian direction that he gave himself a free hand, and introduced, as will presently be shown, arguments which had in them the hectic touch of

European theology rather than the bland, imperturbable acquiescence of the East.

And so, as we read it, this fortunate paraphrase, so full of ease and grace, so supple in its diction and its imagery, makes us forget – as we never forget in reading a translation of Homer or Dante, however good – that it is a translation, and that we are listening at a far remove, to a school of thought much more alien in its mode of expression than the skilful artifice of this version allows us to feel. FitzGerald, by his superlative tact, has done us the favour of deceiving us, making either the East seem West, or the West seem East, in a sympathy of thought and feeling which, at that time, had hardly begun to exist.

But for all its suavity and grace, this gospel of flesh versus spirit, coming in the midst of that very church-going Victorian age, should by its content, one might think, have caused a shock almost as great as Darwin's *Origin of Species* or Swinburne's *Poems and Ballads*. Perhaps being only a translation made its challenge less evident; but there the challenge was; and though for the time thrown down into the rubble of the second-hand book box (price one penny) as a thing too insignificant for notice, its significance grew more apparent as time went on; and when it touches its centenary in 1959, it will almost certainly have lasted better than *In Memoriam*, which – its predecessor by ten years – might in a sense be regarded as the rival oracular pronouncement of that day on the problem of life after death.

For these two poems appeared at a time when, while religious convention was still rampant, religious belief was beginning to seek new supports for the faith that was in it, though the outlook which is now called "modernist" had scarcely begun.

Faith, in the Victorian age (we see it now) was a sort of St. Paul's Cathedral, which – though not perceptibly to the general eye – was beginning to shift on its foundations; and while it still held up an imposing façade, the under-pinning process had already started, and reconstruction was becoming inevitable.

It was at this juncture that these two poems appeared, both of an elegiac character – though it is not as an elegy that the *Rubáiyát* is generally regarded. *In Memoriam*, while incidentally written to commemorate the death of a friend, was in substance an elegy on a disintegrating form of faith, which in Tennyson's estimation could no longer be held by men of open mind, but only by their sisters. And with considerable perturbation of spirit, and not without a certain distrust of that larger hope which he professes, Tennyson lets his weaker sister go to the wall under which she can still find shelter, and builds up for the rest his main thesis that immortality must surely be awaiting us, because it would have been so unfair of God to allow the human race to form false expectations.

The *Rubáiyát* – a more serene, more cheerful, and more contented document – is an elegy on all faiths whatsoever. It states its case with a certain touch of melancholy, but without any cry of distress. Too resigned to be poignant, too philosophical to be bitter about it, it dismisses the dream, and accepts with appetite – almost with gratitude – what is left.

That, at least, seems clearly the thesis of the original. But though FitzGerald keeps up well his western end of it, and makes a brave show of not caring, it is on this very point that, here and there, the influence of his Victorian environment, with its sharpening interrogative, begins to creep in.

> " The Ball no question makes of Ayes and Noes,
>     But Right or Left, as strikes the Player, goes."

There is the good, wise example set before us; but immediately, and in the same stanza, FitzGerald himself departs from it, and asserts very emphatically that there is a Somebody outside who –

> " Knows about it all – He knows – HE knows!"

And then, having asserted the existence of the Knowing One, he proceeds to rub in once more the impotence of human destiny:–

> " With Earth's first Clay They did the Last Man's knead,
>     And then of the Last Harvest sowed the Seed:
>     And the first Morning of Creation wrote
> What the Last Dawn of Reckoning shall read."

And thus launched on the high seas of Calvinism, he goes on further to adumbrate, for indignant protest, the possibility that divine punishment may be in store for those who enjoy life in their own way.

> " What! out of senseless Nothing to provoke
>     A conscious Something to resent the yoke
>         Of unpermitted Pleasure, under pain
> Of Everlasting Penalties, if broke!"

And so – leading up in a crescendo of indignation – to that famous final apostrophe:–

> " Oh, Thou, who Man of baser Earth didst make,
>     And who with Eden didst devise the Snake;
>         For all the Sin wherewith the Face of Man
> Is blacken'd, Man's forgiveness give – and take!"

Now here it is pretty evident that FitzGerald has caused his Omar to stumble against the Deity begotten by the theologians of Geneva; and his voice vibrates with passion, and his war-whoop is the war-whoop of a Victorian letting himself loose, because he has not the far, wise mind which can see ahead for a generation or two, and can afford to be patient and smile over a mirage that has only lasted for a few hundred years.

And so we see that though FitzGerald might be in revolt against the theology of his day, he could not indifferently escape it as though it did not exist. His Persian carpet was not so magic as to waft him away entirely from his "suburb grange" to the singing rose gardens of Naishápúr.

But for all that he gave to English literature something that was new, beautiful, and permanent. Steadily through changing schools of expression, and changing interest in matters of technique, the form of expression here chosen has commended itself to minds differently trained, differently attuned, and still to its purpose seems perfect.

More than that: it would be difficult to name any single poem – long or short – written during the last hundred years which has so taken hold of the thought of succeeding generations, not necessarily for agreement with its ethical content, but for recognition. To a thesis which, without it, might have seemed soulless – materialism run to seed – it has given a dignity, a grace, and a logical force which "orthodoxy" must reckon with. It is harder than it was formerly to damn a man theologically for believing that, in this life, life as we see it is the only true guide.

> " For in the Market-place, one Dusk of Day,
> I watch'd the Potter thumping his wet Clay;
> And with its all obliterated Tongue
> It murmur'd, 'Gently, Brother, gently, pray!'

> " And has not such a story from of old
> Down Man's successive generations rolled
> Of such a clod of saturated Earth
> Cast by the Maker into Human mould?"

The argument is too humanly persuasive for our minds to escape from it. Without believing so much in the Potter – or pretending to know so much about Him as did the theologians of Geneva – here is a writer, a divine, who helps us to think better of Him, and to be sure – if He exists – that He is not so black as the theologians have painted him.

But while he gives us this certificate of the Potter's good character, and His kindly treatment of the clay – as clay, it is but a negative goodness of which he assures us; and that, some are inclined to think, is not enough for the Potter Himself to rest content with.

That is the crucial point where the philosophy of Omar and FitzGerald stops short; they make a guess that the Potter exists, but they don't quite like to guess that He is as good as they are – and as interested in life. And so, while the Ayes and the Noes of this problem of human existence still entangle them more than they are aware, the Noes generally have it; and it is significant, I think, that at the one point in the whole poem where FitzGerald breaks form, and, for the sake of added emphasis, inserts a redundant rhyme, the word he goes out of his way to insert is – "Lies."

> " Oh, come with old Khayyám, and leave the Wise
>     To talk; one thing at least is certain, that Life flies:
>         One thing is certain and the Rest is Lies;
>     The Flower that once has blown for ever dies."

There is an honest man overstating his case. Tennyson had a "larger hope" which he did not call a certainty; but he was not a liar for holding it. I myself am more inclined to share the doubts of FitzGerald and Omar than the hopes of Tennyson, but I am by no means sure about it. Also the Potter may be improving in the manipulation of His material. Who knows? We have the authority of FitzGerald for saying that the Potter Himself knows. If, then, the Potter is really improving in His craft, something more may come of it; we may even come to share His knowledge, without being adjudged "liars."

*Laurence Housman*

For like a Child sent with a fluttering Light
To feel his way along a gusty Night
Man walks the World: again and yet again
The Lamp shall be by Fits of Passion slain:
But shall not He who sent him from the Door
Relight the Lamp once more, and yet once more?

from the *Mantik-ut-tair*, or
*Parliament of Birds* by Attár.
(FitzGerald's translation.)

# EDWARD FITZGERALD

## THE MAN

EDWARD PURCELL, the seventh of a family of eight children, three of whom were boys, was born on March 31st, 1809, at Bredfield House, a late Jacobean building standing in its own park of sixty-five acres, near Woodbridge, Suffolk. His father, John Purcell, was the son of a wealthy Irish doctor. His mother, Mary Frances FitzGerald Purcell, also came of a well-to-do family, and when her father died in 1818 leaving her the whole of his fortune, her husband assumed the name of FitzGerald. They had married in 1801 and were first cousins. The family lived in great splendour; they had a town house in London, at least four estates in the country, and at the age of seven Edward enjoyed the advantages of spending two years partly in Saint-Germain-en-Laye and partly in Paris. When twelve years of age he was sent to King Edward VI Grammar School, Bury St. Edmunds, and in 1826, when he was seventeen, he went up to Trinity College, Cambridge. From 1826 until 1835 the family lived at Wherstead Lodge, which stands on high ground overlooking the river Orwell some two miles south of Ipswich, and during those years Edward was a familiar figure in the town. His favourite haunt was the second-hand book shop kept by James Read, who supplied him with fuel for the mind and the imagination and became his lifelong friend.

FitzGerald had an engaging personality which found expression in the tastes of the patrician, the way of life of the scholar and the habits of the bohemian. He was too much the individualist ever to become blighted by respectability, but a delicate fastidiousness kept him aloof from undergraduate dissipation. He had all the money one could wish for, but would seem to have spent little on himself.

15

One pictures him during those four years at Cambridge in the serenity and beauty of an environment in which he could indulge his tastes as the spirit moved him, for, being well provided for, he had neither ambition nor goal. He read discursively but extensively, wrote some poetry, played the piano, painted in water colours, or just lazed. He was habitually untidy, shaved as seldom as possible, dressed as he pleased, and his rooms were constantly littered with clothes, books, music, pictures, pipes and what not. But he was a delightful companion and had in course of time a wide circle of friends among whom were W. M. Thackeray, F. D. Morris, John Kemble, W. B. Donne, Richard Monckton Milnes (later Lord Houghton) and James Spedding. Later he was to write of Alfred Tennyson: "I remember him well – a sort of Hyperion": that they did not meet when undergraduates was probably due to FitzGerald's shyness and indifference. His enthusiasm for Tennyson's poetry, at first impersonal, grew with their friendship. Some years later he wrote to John Allen: "I will say no more of Tennyson than that the more I have seen of him, the more cause I have to think him great."

He took his degree with modest competence in February 1830, and left the University to spend the springtime of the year in Paris, where, on the arrival of the truant Thackeray from Cambridge, the threat of boredom gave place to the carefree and unselfconscious exhilaration of kindred spirits enthralled by the delights of novel experiences perfectly shared together. On his return to England he spent most of the summer at Southampton and the remainder of the year in London, Suffolk and elsewhere, and in the years that followed he was again and again irresistibly drawn to Cambridge.

The family took up residence at Boulge Hall in 1835 and Edward chose, from 1837 onwards, to live during the summer months in a thatched cottage of two rooms standing just outside the park gates. Spring, summer, autumn, winter – sixteen years advanced and dwindled in long, untragic crescendos and diminuendos. But FitzGerald was not wholly idle. He interested himself in the

2/71

management of his father's estates, read widely and omnivorously of whatever his mind craved for, bought pictures, wrote for his own pleasure, entertained, and was entertained by, his friends. And if he could remark to Frederick Tennyson: "Here I sit, read, smoke, and become very wise, and am already quite beyond earthly needs," it should be remembered to his credit that in an age when the social conscience was little stirred by the poverty of the masses, he was deeply concerned about the penury and suffering he saw about him and did what he could to assuage such evils.

On his father's death in 1853 the Hall passed to his elder brother John, who suffered from religious mania. He is said to have roamed about the country, preaching wherever he could find an audience. When listening to a sermon he would remove his shoes and stockings, empty his pockets of their contents and give vent to his emotion by emitting shrill whistles. "We FitzGeralds are all mad," Edward used to say, "but John is the maddest for he does not know it," and this may explain his decision to leave the cottage and lodge with his friend Job Smith in the picturesque farmhouse of Farlingay on the outskirts of Woodbridge. Farlingay Hall was his home until 1860 – it was here that Carlyle paid him a visit in 1855 – but his was a restless spirit, and although he never travelled abroad, he could not remain in one place for any length of time. During those years he made frequent visits to London, to his brother Peter at Twickenham, his sister Andalusia at Bath and his mother at Richmond, until her death in Brighton in 1855. He went on visits to friends for months at a time, preferring their warm hospitality to the more forbidding atmosphere of hotels or the purlieus of the family. He detested the pomp and circumstance of the court and officialdom and the spurious glamour of the social scene. For him such activities were unsubstantial and alien to the spirit, and he had no need of them. What he required was freedom to express his many-sided personality with genuine bonhomie and spontaneity, and he was probably happiest of all when lodged in friendly detachment nearby simple country people.

Among his close friends in Woodbridge was the banker and Quaker poet Bernard Barton who was some twenty-five years his senior. In the course of Barton's last illness in 1849 FitzGerald had given an assurance that he would make provision for his daughter Lucy, and a death-bed incident in which her father joined his daughter's and FitzGerald's hands and gave the pair his blessing would seem to have been interpreted by FitzGerald as an unformulated but none the less unambiguous directive. It is probable that his original intention was simply to make Lucy an allowance to supplement her slender income, but this her sense of propriety forbade her to accept. As time went on FitzGerald became increasingly conscious of his 'obligation,' but his father's bankruptcy involved him in financial difficulties which for a time made marriage inadvisable. These ended on the death of his mother. He inherited a fortune, and, disregarding the protestations of his friends, Lucy and he were married on November 4th, 1856 – seven years after her father's death.

As the twig is bent, so is the tree inclined, and that the marriage was a failure was soon apparent in ever growing unhappiness and incompatibility. In a letter to Spring Rice, FitzGerald had described his forthcoming marriage as "a very doubtful experiment", and to Crabbe he wrote: "George, I am going to be married – don't congratulate me." The plain truth is that FitzGerald was not the marrying kind; no two mortals could have been more unsuited to each other. He was too ascetic in temperament, too eccentric in his habits, too settled in his bachelor ways ever to accommodate himself to such a loveless union. His wife was too precise, too respectable, too confirmed in her determination to reform her husband's manners and way of life. In the words of F. R. Barton: "the more she tried in her fond, tactless way to win his regard, the more she repelled him." On the other hand, she could hardly have been expected to conform to the pact which FitzGerald made before they were married: "to see no company, to keep no establishment, and to live very quietly." As everyone had foreseen, the situation was irremediable, but there was no divorce. In August 1857 they agreed to separate permanently and FitzGerald made Lucy a generous settlement.

"You know well enough," he wrote to a friend, "that *I* am very much to blame, both on the score of stupidity in taking so wrong a step, and want of courageous principle in not making the best of it when taken. She has little to blame herself for, except in fancying that she knew both me and herself better than I had over and over again told her was the truth *before* marriage." Or again (in a letter to Mrs. Tennyson): "If people want to go further for the cause of all this Blunder than the fact of two People of very determined habits and Temper, first trying to change them at close on fifty – you may lay nine-tenths of the blame on me." Lucy, who, in common with FitzGerald, was forty-eight years of age at the time of her marriage, died at Croydon in 1898 at the age of ninety.

In December 1860, FitzGerald removed to lodgings at Berry's, a Gunsmith's shop on the Market Hill, Woodbridge, where he lived until 1873. He must have known that his reputation was that of an eccentric. Furthermore, he had been parted from his wife for three years and it required considerable moral courage thus boldly to face the gossips of the town, to whom she was a well-known and popular figure. He shunned Woodbridge society but made many friends among the townspeople, and although he took little part in civic affairs, he was not unmindful of those in need and found ways and means quietly to distribute his benefactions. It required something more than mere eccentricity to burn the bond for £500 which Frederick Spalding's father and a friend had signed so that the son might establish a business. That was the act of a generous and big-hearted man.

FitzGerald loved the sea. Tentative beginnings with river boats and a passage to Berwick-on-Tweed in a smack during the summer of 1861 led him to experiment with larger craft and, in 1863, to the building of his yacht *Shamrock*, the which, however, was soon rechristened *Scandal*, that being "the staple product of Woodbridge." How exhilarating he must have found those summer coastal cruises from Lowestoft during the ensuing eight years. A friend or two with whom to read poetry and share the wisdom of great minds; a cold pasty and a bottle of sherry, or the more humble bread and cheese and ale, for the needs of the body: "the flung spray and the blown spume, and the sea-gulls crying." What more, short of paradise, could one of his temperament have wished for?

In the spring of 1864 FitzGerald made the acquaintance of Joseph Fletcher a Lowestoft fisherman, for whom he soon had a great affection. Tall and strong and native to the sea, 'Posh' was a bearded giant of sturdy independence and simplicity of character and, as is so often the case in men endowed with great physical strength, his gentleness and guileless humour were quite disarming. "The Greatest Man I have known," wrote FitzGerald, and they became firm friends. Indeed for a time (1867–1873) they were partners in a fishing lugger, the *Meum et Tuum*. "So now," he wrote to Spalding, "I shall be very glad to drop the *Esquire*, and to be addressed as 'Herring-Merchant' for the future." The venture brought FitzGerald no monetary gain, but it earned him dividends infinitely more precious in the coin of human values and experience.

As was inevitable in such a relationship there were disappointments, misunderstandings brought about by interfering busybodies, recriminations and estrangements, but nothing could quite sever the bond between the friends. Even when their business relationship had foundered, FitzGerald commissioned Lawrence to paint 'Posh's' portrait "to hang up by old Thackeray and Tennyson, all three having a stamp of grandeur about them in their several ways, and occupying great places in my Soul." 'Posh's' opinion of FitzGerald can be summed up in a single sentence: "Ah! He was a master rum un, was my ole guv'nor!"

In 1864 FitzGerald bought the Little Grange, an estate of about six acres on the outskirts of Woodbridge. A year later he had the house enlarged and refurnished, but although he loaned it occasionally to his Kerrich nieces and to some of his friends, he himself did not move in until the spring of 1874. This was his last home. He was, as always, stubborn in his resolve to have nothing to do with 'the County,' but he continued to be a jovial and voluminous correspondent, and the visits of Sir Frederick Pollock, Frederick Tennyson and many others of his friends, the English summers at Lowestoft and elsewhere, and his brief visits to London, all brought him keen enjoyment.

In 1876 he was surprised and delighted to receive a visit from Alfred Tennyson and his son Hallam. The Tennysons had been touring in Norfolk and were on their way back to London. Little Grange was in the hands of the painters and his guests were lodged in the Bull Hotel on the Market Hill. Twenty years had elapsed since their last meeting, and now, during this brief interlude of two days, they yarned about old friends and re-lived experiences they had shared together. There were times when he found the great man a little overpowering, but nothing could suppress FitzGerald's native buoyancy – "Tennyson's little humours and grumpiness were so droll that I was always laughing" – and both felt in parting the pangs of their last farewell. And Tennyson's opinion of FitzGerald? "I had no truer friend: he was one of the kindliest of men, and I have never known one of so fine and delicate a wit."

The remaining years of FitzGerald's life were overshadowed with quiet melancholy. He was much saddened by the death of friends and relatives but, stooping a little, he carried his years with stubborn and ungraceful vigour. His mind was as lively as ever, and he was constantly occupied with one project and another, including a third edition of *Euphranor*. That he left unfinished at least three books on which he had been working off and on prior to his death, belies his self-accusation that he was lacking in industry.

Even death was kind to him, for he passed quietly in sleep at Merton Rectory on June 14th, 1883, while on his annual visit to his friend the Rev. George Crabbe, grandson of the poet. He was seventy-four. His body was interred on June 19th in the little churchyard in Boulge Park, and there grows the famous rose tree the hips for which were picked by William Simpson from rose bushes on the grave of Omar Khayyám in Naishápúr in 1884, and raised at Kew Gardens before being planted at Boulge in 1893.

But of what avail is it to garner and patch and seam, for not thus shall we recapture the soul of the poet. His whimsical and eccentric personality, that part of him which was incorrigibly fond of mimicry and drollery, is perhaps best revealed in his letters, but Francis Hindes Groome has brought to life the figure which was so familiar to the village gossips: "I can see him now walking down to Woodbridge with an old Inverness cape, double-breasted flowered satin waistcoat, slippers on feet and a handkerchief, very likely, tied over his hat. Yet one always recognised in him the Hidalgo." But life does not consist of outward acts and is little affected by them: it is an inward and subjective experience. The real FitzGerald, the creative artist who abridged, concentrated and distilled the work of the Persian master, escapes us, save what we glimpse of him in the *Rubáiyát* of our own perception and awareness.

# THE WORKS OF FITZGERALD

## 1

## *Earlier Ventures in Publishing*

The first printed work by FitzGerald, *Euphranor, A Dialogue on Youth* in the Platonic manner, was published in 1851 when he was forty-two. It mirrors in the somewhat thin disguise of classical nomenclature the author's collegiate life and associations during his undergraduate sojourn at Cambridge, and while its serious purpose is to criticise the English system of education of that day, its whimsical and kindly philosophy is spun from a mind to which old ties of custom and friendship were both hallowed and enduring. In 1852 there appeared *Polonius, A Collection of Wise Saws and Modern*

*Instances*. This consisted of short moral aphorisms and larger excerpts arranged under abstract headings, some original, the rest derived from English, French and German classical sources, and even from the Persian of the *Masnavi*, evidence of the beginning of FitzGerald's interest in this field of literature. In general the book reflects the wide range of his reading, and that it contains a disproportionate number of quotations from Carlyle is testimony to still another of his close friendships. This book (in common with *Euphranor*) was published at his own expense and met with small success. Turning his attention to Spain, he published in the following year a translation in free blank verse of *Six Dramas of Calderon* (1600–1681) whom he thought to be "one of the Great Men of the World," a volume which, in spite of its considerable merit, had so unfavourable a reception that he felt obliged to withdraw it from circulation. This was the first and indeed the only book to bear his name, for he would never again consent to use it.

In the course of his pilgrimages to Cambridge in middle life, FitzGerald became friendly with Edward Byles Cowell, an Oriental scholar of distinction and a man of great personal charm and modesty. Cowell was then at Oxford, but he left England in 1856 to become Professor of History at the new Presidency College, and soon after Principal of the Sanskrit College, Calcutta, and did not return until 1867 when he was elected Professor of Sanskrit at Cambridge. Cowell quickened and fostered FitzGerald's interest in his Persian studies, which began with Háfiz "whose best is untranslatable because he is the best Musician of Words," and in a letter to Frederick Tennyson in 1853 is found this sentence: "I amuse myself with poking out some Persian, which E. Cowell would inaugurate me with; I go on with it because it is a point in common with him and enables us to study a little together." Thus it came about that in 1856 there appeared anonymously FitzGerald's version of the Sufi allegorical work *Salámán and Absál* by Jámi, which, despite certain weaknesses in translation, deserved a better reception than was accorded to it.

This literary exercise he was to find invaluable for his work on Omar.

Furthermore, that FitzGerald understood something of the inner significance of the work is evident from the following observation in a letter to Cowell: " 'Salaman and Absal' is one of many Allegories under which the Persian Mystic symbolized an esoteric doctrine which he dared not – and probably could not – more intelligibly reveal." As always FitzGerald made a free rather than a literal translation. His abridgement he thought to be a gain and advantageous to western minds, and he considered this work to be the best of his translations from the Persian.

In 1876 he produced a version of the *Agamemnon* of Æschylus in which, too, he strove to capture the spirit of the original rather than to give a too literal rendering. In 1880–81 he issued for private circulation translations of the two Œdipus tragedies, which are full of poetic beauty. His last publication, *Readings in Crabbe* (which had been privately distributed in 1879) appeared in 1882 and is interesting primarily as a gesture of friendship to the poet's grandson.

2

## *Rubáiyát of Omar Khayyám*

The original manuscript by Omar Khayyám is thought to have comprised at least seven hundred and fifty and possibly many more quatrains. These were never intended to represent a continuous work or story. Each quatrain is a separate poem, the epigrammatic expression of a single thought about such subjects as would occur to the mind of a Persian poet-philosopher, and, moreover, one skilled in mathematics and astronomy. The *Rubáiyát* are the expression of Omar's own life, the fruits of his own experience, and they were not written for publication.

Of this large and varied collection, the Ouseley manuscript discovered by Cowell among a mass of uncatalogued material in the Bodleian Library, Oxford, in 1856, contains 158 quatrains written in purple ink on yellow paper and powdered in gold. It dates from 865, (i.e. A.D. 1460–61,) some 338 years after the death of Omar. From the transcript which he made from Cowell's copy of the original, FitzGerald selected and compounded for his first edition of the *Rubáiyát* seventy-five quatrains, on which he worked for several years. By the middle of 1857 he had finished his 'first Physiognomy' and the following year he wrote to Cowell: "My translation will interest you from its form, and also in many respects in its detail, very unliteral as it is. Many quatrains are mashed together, and something lost, I doubt, of Omar's simplicity, which is such a virtue in him. But there it is, such as it is."

The 'less wicked' of the quatrains FitzGerald sent to Parker of *Fraser's Magazine* in January 1858, but when a year had elapsed and nothing had been published, he recalled the manuscript, replaced the 'wicked' stanzas and resolved to print it for private circulation. Thus there appeared in the early summer of 1859 the quarto pamphlet of twenty-four pages in its unassuming brown paper cover, "Beggarly disguise as to paper and print, but magnificent vesture of verse."

A comparative examination of translations from the Persian original, and especially that of the "Teheran" manuscript dated 604, (i.e. A.D. 1207,) which was acquired by Cambridge University Library in 1950, translated by Professor Arthur J. Arberry and published in 1952, makes clear that FitzGerald did not so much translate Omar as make a poetic transfusion of the quatrains to suit his own fancy. This he did with such skill and beauty that some have thought his work incomparably better than the original, but he took great liberties with the text. About half of the quatrains are faithful paraphrases of the Persian. The remainder are built up of ideas taken from this quatrain and that, of figures which have no prototypes in the original but come from numerous kindred sources such as Háfiz and the *Mantik-ut-Tair* (*The Parliament of Birds*) of Attár. However the whole underwent so singular a poetic metamorphosis that FitzGerald's rendering is justly considered the apotheosis of craftsmanship – but it is not Omar.

In a letter to Cowell dated 27th April, 1859, he wrote: "I hardly know why I print any of these things, which nobody buys; and I scarce now see the few I gave them to. But when one has done one's best, and is sure that the best is better than so many will take pains to do, though far from the best that might be done, one likes to make an end of the matter by print. I suppose very few people have ever taken such pains in translation as I have, though certainly not to be literal." And again: "It is a desperate sort of thing, unfortunately at the bottom of all thinking men's minds, but made music of." It is this music, coupled with the seemingly dark philosophy of the *Rubáiyát*, that continues to enthral the western world.

## 3

## *Exoteric or Esoteric?*

There are two schools of thought about the *Rubáiyát*. The first contends that FitzGerald recaptured and expressed with admirable restraint and superb poetic imagery the thoughts of Omar on love and wine, and life and death, and this notwithstanding that he destroyed the verisimilitude of the work by too many borrowings, too free renderings, and by giving it a continuity that does not exist in the original. Omar's, say the adherents of this school, was a materialist philosophy which could be summed up in a single epigram: "Eat, drink and be merry, for to-morrow we die." It is hard indeed to fit this interpretation to many of the quatrains even in FitzGerald's renderings, but it is fair to say that this was his own opinion, that it is Professor Arberry's opinion and that it is the opinion of the majority. It does not follow, of course, that it is the right one. How, for example, shall we attribute other than a mystical interpretation to Quatrain 34 in FitzGerald's fifth edition of the *Rubáiyát*?

> Then of the THEE IN ME who works behind
> The Veil, I lifted up my hands to find
>     A lamp amid the Darkness; and I heard,
> As from Without – "THE ME WITHIN THEE BLIND!"

No corresponding quatrain is found in the Cambridge codex, and it must be admitted that of its 252 quatrains hardly any can be said to bear evidence of mystical teaching; but that Omar was not unaware of such is hinted at in the quatrains which Professor Arberry translates as follows:

> The secrets of the world, as we
>     Succinctly on our tablets write,
>     Are not expedient to recite:
> A plague to heart and head they be.

> Since there is none, as I can find,
>     Of those brave wizards of today
>     Worthy to hear, I cannot say
> The wondrous thoughts I have in mind.

Or again:

> Lord, I am weary unto death
>     Of this mean being that is mine:
>     The fetters that my heart confine,
> My muddy hands, my narrow breath.

    Yet Thou hast power to transmute
    The naughted unto entity:
    O raise me to the sanctuary
Of Thine own Being Absolute.

The other school, which began with the Moslem mystics and was revived by M. Nicolas, Omar's French translator, claims that Omar was a philosopher who was concerned primarily with spiritual values, a man going his own way in solitude, appealed to by others but independent of their thought; moreover, a man passionate in revolt against the fixed ideas of his age. For them the *Rubáiyát*, in translations which were formerly thought to be more faithful to the original, must be given a spiritual interpretation. In other words, they have an allegorical significance.

This would seem to have been the opinion of Sharastani (A.D. 1074–1153) a dogmatic theologian of the Asharite sect and a distinguished doctor of law who lived for a time in Naishápúr, and paid tribute to Omar as the greatest scholar of his time, one versed in the philosophy and political theory of the Greeks, and who exhorted men to seek the One Author of all by the purification of the senses and the sanctification of the soul. He confirms the modern view that Omar found in the orthodox Sufism of his day much that was repugnant to him and hints plainly that the verses have an esoteric significance. "The later Sufis," he wrote, "have caught at the apparent sense of parts of his poems and accommodated them to their own canon, making them a subject of discussion in their assemblies and conventicles, but the esoteric sense consists in axioms of natural religion and principles of universal obligation. When the men of his time anathematised his doctrines, and drew forth his opinions from the concealment in which he had veiled them, he went in fear of his life and placed some check on the sallies of his tongue and pen." Thus, not for the first or last time in the world's history, a great scholar and thinker, on whom had fallen the mantle of Avicenna, versed in philosophy, science, mathematics, astronomy and medicine, found it expedient to conform to the orthodox philosophical dialetic of the age, to put away his pen, put a rein on his tongue, and to make pilgrimage to Mecca.

We are asked, then, to distinguish between Omar's own high philosophy and the spurious and decadent Sufism of his day, and to regard him as a great satirist, to be ranked with Lucian and Carlyle. If we probe behind the symbol or metaphor, we shall discover a noble philosophy which will guide us through the mysteries of life and destiny.

The Tavern or Caravanserai is symbolic of Pilgrimage, the Sufi way of Life with its five stages of Repentance, Renunciation, Poverty, Patience and Acquiescence to the Will of God. The Temple is a thing of Time which, when it has served its purpose, will pass away; not so the Temple of the Dweller in the Heart. Wine is symbolic of the Spirit; the Cup the receptacle of the Spiritual powers poured out in Service: Bread the Divine Mind or Food from Heaven; the Bulbul or Persian Nightingale the Symbol of the Soul, singing in the darkness or hidden depths of man's own being. And so on.

It is evident that, be the quatrains secular or mystical, their form and significance in English must depend upon the wisdom and skill of the translator. It would be foolish to suppose that *all*, or indeed the majority, have a mystical significance. The correct verdict on the evidence is that, in so large and varied an anthology, some reflect in symbolic language the inner philosophy of the spirit, while others are epigrammatic expressions of the mundane.

The reader who is interested may pursue his investigations and sift the evidences to form his own judgment by examining versions such as those of Professor Arthur J. Arberry, John Leslie Garner, E. H. Whinfield and the French of M. Nicolas, or he may decide to rest satisfied with the FitzGerald rendering. This is so felicitous, so Schubert-like in the excellence of its poetry, that it will always find a readier response among English-speaking peoples than the more literal, though excellent, prose translations of Justin Huntly McCarthy and Edward Heron-Allan.

## 4

## *Comparative Translations*

It is interesting to compare one of the FitzGerald quatrains with that of other translators, and I have chosen for this purpose Quatrain 77 from the fifth edition of the *Rubáiyát*; which reads:

> And this I know: whether the one True Light
> Kindle to Love, or Wrath-consume me quite,
>   One flash of It within the Tavern caught
> Better than in the Temple lost outright.

In the metrical version by E. H. Whinfield this quatrain reads:

> In taverns better far commune with Thee,
> Than pray in mosques and fail Thy face to see!
>   O first and last of all Thy creatures Thou;
> 'Tis Thine to burn, and Thine to cherish me!

That by Brigadier-General E. H. Rodwell, C.B., reads:

> In some low Inn I'd rather seek Thy face
> Than pray without Thee towards the Niche's place.
>   O First and Last of all! As Thou dost will,
> Burn me in Hell – or save me by Thy grace!

That by Professor A. J. Arberry (in his translation of the Cambridge manuscript) reads:

> Better at tavern, and with wine,
>     To lay Thee all my secrets bare,
>     Than to intone the parrot prayer
> And Thou not with me, in the shrine.
>
> Thy Name is last and first to tell;
>     Whatever is, save Thee, is nil;
>     Then cherish me, if so Thy Will
> Be done – or burn my soul in hell!

Compare the literal prose version of the same quatrain by Justin Huntly McCarthy:

> I would rather in the tavern with Thee pour out
> all the thoughts of my heart, than without Thee
> go and make my prayer unto Heaven. This, truly,
> O creator of all things present and to come, is
> my religion; whether Thou castest me into the
> flames, or makest me glad with the light of
> Thy countenance.

There follows the version of Edward Heron-Allen:

> If I tell Thee my secret thoughts in a tavern,
> it is better than if I make my devotions before
>     the Mihráb without Thee.
> O Thou, the first and last of all created beings!
> burn me an Thou wilt, or cherish me an Thou wilt.

No quatrain has caused more controversy than that numbered 68 in FitzGerald's fifth edition of the *Rubáiyát*:

> We are no other than a moving row
> Of Magic Shadow-shapes that come and go
>   Round with the Sun-illumined Lantern held
> In Midnight by the Master of the Show.

According to Dr. Richard Ettinghausen, writing in the bulletin of the American Institute for Persian Art and Archaeology, "The poet speaks of a lamp with a revolving shade on which figures are painted, for him a symbol of human life, the purposeless movement of men and the all-moving power. . . . Such a lantern is made of paper in the form and size of a bucket; on its surface strange comical looking figures are painted. Inside the lanterns, which are hung up before the shops, are wax candles which, by the heat of their flames, cause the shade to move round incessantly so that new figures appear."

The Heron-Allen rendering of the same rubái reads:

> This vault of heaven, beneath which we stand bewildered,
> We know to be a sort of magic-lantern:
> Know thou that the sun is the lamp-flame and
>   the universe is the lamp,
> We are the figures that revolve round it.

Did Omar know that the earth revolves in space and travels round the sun, and that the solar system describes a still greater orbit? The ancient Egyptians possessed this knowledge. May not the wise men of the East have been similarly enlightened?

1/1

5

## *The Five FitzGerald Transcriptions*

Until the end of his life FitzGerald kept working on the *Rubáiyát*, adding to or reducing the number of quatrains, changing their order, their phrasing, striving for a perfection that for ever eluded him. Four versions were published anonymously during his lifetime. The first, to which I have referred, containing seventy-five quatrains, appeared in 1859. The second edition, that of 1868, contained one hundred and ten, but in the third and fourth editions which appeared in 1872 and 1879 respectively, the number of quatrains was reduced to one hundred and one. On his death, his friend William Aldis Wright found in a tin box a printed copy of the 1879 text in which FitzGerald had marked some further changes. This, the fifth and last revision, was incorporated in *Letters and Literary Remains of Edward FitzGerald* (3 vols.) published in 1889, when for the first time his name appeared as the author of the *Rubáiyát*. The present volume gives the first, second and fifth editions of the *Rubáiyát* in full, together with the variations in the texts of the third and fourth editions.

The work aroused as little enthusiasm in the country of its adoption as it had done in the country of its origin in the eleventh century. It is a sobering reflection that, thanks to Thomas Sergeant Perry, a distinguished critic, editor and teacher, it was widely read and appreciated in the United States of America long before it became popular fare in this country, largely because of the reactionary mode of thought which followed upon the Civil War. When, however, in 1885 Tennyson dedicated *Tiresias and other Poems* to the memory of FitzGerald, there began in Great Britain an awakening of interest in the *Rubáiyát* which has grown to such proportions that it is now known and quoted wherever English is spoken.

O.K.                                                                                                  C

## 6

### *Advent in English*

The manner of its advent is not without interest. In the year 1861 the more perceptive among those who are forever drawn to second-hand book stalls as the magnetic needle to the pole, bought at a penny a piece a pamphlet which bore the title: *Rubáiyát of Omar Khayyám the Astronomer-Poet of Persia, Translated into English Verse.* The name of the translator was not disclosed. In 1859 Bernard Quaritch the bookseller had had printed for the author two hundred and fifty copies, of which FitzGerald retained forty for his friends. The majority of these were never distributed, but he gave copies to Cowell, who "was naturally alarmed at it, he being a very religious man," to George Borrow and to Donne. The remainder he gifted to his publisher. These were advertised in Quaritch's Catalogue No. 158, dated March 15th, 1860, at 1s., with a notice from the *Literary Gazette* of October 1859, but the work aroused little interest, and as none foresaw that it was destined to become a best-seller, it was progressively reduced in price until it found its way into 'the penny box.' Indeed had not Rossetti and Swinburne got wind of this singular second-hand bargain, the bulk of the first edition would probably have been disposed of as waste-paper. Soon this 'remainder' was being sold at ever-increasing prices, until a guinea and more was paid for single copies. To-day its value to the collector is such that a copy sold in the U.S.A. in 1929 fetched eight thousand dollars, and another was sold by Hodgson's in London on June 12th the same year for £1410.

It has been said that happiness consists of having something to love, something to do, and something to hope for. FitzGerald loved his friends by whom he was held in warm affection as an amiable and kindly spirit, an affection which, overcoming time and circumstance, has attained immortality. That he enjoyed his literary work, and in particular that on the *Rubáiyát*, is plain from the fact that he returned to it again and again. Did he hope that this, the best-loved of his creations, would one day achieve the world-wide popularity which it now enjoys? Surely the answer must be that one who was so modest as to choose the cloak of anonymity had no such mundane hope, and that the *Rubáiyát* was the offspring of labours that gave wings to his soul.

In a letter to his friend Cowell he wrote: "June over! a thing I think of with Omar-like sorrow, and the roses here are blooming – and going – as abundantly as even in Persia. I am still at Geldestone, and still looking at Omar by an open window, which gives over a greener landscape than yours."

> Rain, sun and Rain! and the free blossom blows:
> Sun, rain and Sun! and where is he who knows?
> From the great deep to the great deep he goes.
>                                          *G. F. Maine.*

# NOTE

The earliest known reference to Omar Khayyám in the western world is found in "*De Emendatione Temporum*" (First edition, Basle, 1583; Second edition, Geneva, 1629, p. 304) by the eminent scholar Joseph Scaliger, the founder of modern chronology. As far as can be traced, the first translation into English of any portion of the Rubáiyát appears in a work edited by Von Hammer Purgstall and published in Vienna in 1816. This contains amongst other Oriental literature, two quatrains translated by H. G. Keene.

The earliest known Persian manuscript is the "Teheran" which is dated 604 (A.D. 1207). It was acquired by Cambridge University Library in 1950, translated by Arthur J. Arberry, Sir Thomas Adams Professor of Arabic in the University of Cambridge, and published in 1952. It contains 252 quatrains.

Readers who wish to enlarge their knowledge of the life and times of Omar should read *Persian Mosaic*, the American title of which is *Omar Khayyám, a Life: an imaginative Biography of Omar Khayyám, Based upon Reality in the Oriental manner*, by Harrold Lamb. Mr. Lamb, who is well grounded in the Persian language and medieval Persian history, has done a magnificent job of historical reconstruction, the product of a fine and sensitive imagination.

There was published in 1947 *The Life of Edward FitzGerald* by Alfred McKinley Terhune. This, the first full life to be written with the approval of the FitzGerald family, is an indispensable source book on FitzGerald as a personality and literary artist and contains a wealth of information about his contemporaries.

Another book of unusual interest (published 1950) is *Into an Old Room: The Paradox of Edward FitzGerald* by Peter de Polnay. The author lived for two years in Boulge Hall, evoked, so to speak, the shade of FitzGerald, and this feeling for his subject, linked to genuine research, produced the best interpretive biography of FitzGerald.

# OMAR KHAYYÁM

OMAR KHAYYÁM was born at Naishápúr in Khorásán in
the latter half of our Eleventh, and died within the first
Quarter of our Twelfth Century. The slender Story of his Life is
curiously twined about that of two other very considerable Figures
in their Time and Country: one of whom tells the Story of all
Three. This was Nizám-ul-Mulk, Vizier to Alp Arslan the Son, and
Malik Shah the Grandson, of Toghrul Beg the Tartar, who had
wrested Persia from the feeble Successor of Mahmud the Great,
and founded that Seljukian Dynasty which finally roused Europe
into the Crusades. This Nizám-ul-Mulk, in his *Wasiyat* – or
*Testament* – which he wrote and left as a Memorial for future
Statesmen – relates the following, as quoted in the *Calcutta Review*,
No. 59, from Mirkhond's *History of the Assassins*.

"One of the greatest of the wise men of Khorásán was the
Imám Mowaffak of Naishápúr, a man highly honoured and
reverenced, – may God rejoice his soul; his illustrious years
exceeded eighty-five, and it was the universal belief that every
boy who read the Koran or studied the traditions in his presence,
would assuredly attain to honour and happiness. For this cause
did my father send me from Tús to Naishápúr with Abd-us-
samad, the doctor of law, that I might employ myself in study
and learning under the guidance of that illustrious teacher.
Towards me he ever turned an eye of favour and kindness, and as
his pupil I felt for him extreme affection and devotion, so that I
passed four years in his service. When I first came there, I found
two other pupils of mine own age newly arrived, Hakim Omar
Khayyám, and the ill-fated Ben Sabbáh. Both were endowed

with sharpness of wit and the highest natural powers; and we three formed a close friendship together. When the Imám rose from his lectures, they used to join me, and we repeated to each other the lessons we had heard. Now Omar was a native of Naishápúr, while Hasan Ben Sabbáh's father was one Ali, a man of austere life and practice, but heretical in his creed and doctrine. One day Hasan said to me and to Khayyám, 'It is a universal belief that the pupils of the Imám Mowaffak will attain to fortune. Now, even if we *all* do not attain thereto, without doubt one of us will; what then shall be our mutual pledge and bond?' We answered, 'Be it what you please.' 'Well,' he said, 'let us make a vow, that to whomsoever this fortune falls, he shall share it equally with the rest, and reserve no pre-eminence for himself.' 'Be it so,' we both replied, and on those terms we mutually pledged our words. Years rolled on, and I went from Khorásán to Transoxiana, and wandered to Ghazni and Cabul; and when I returned, I was invested with office, and rose to be administrator of affairs during the Sultanate of Sultán Alp Arslan.

"He goes on to state, that years passed by, and both his old school-friends found him out, and came and claimed a share in his good fortune, according to the school-day vow. The Vizier was generous and kept his word. Hasan demanded a place in the government, which the Sultán granted at the Vizier's request; but discontented with a gradual rise, he plunged into the maze of intrigue of an oriental court, and, failing in a base attempt to supplant his benefactor, he was disgraced and fell. After many mishaps and wanderings, Hasan became the head of the Persian sect of the *Ismailians*, – a party of fanatics who had long murmured in obscurity, but rose to an evil eminence under the guidance of his strong and evil will. In A.D. 1090, he seized the castle of Alamút, in the province of Rúdbar, which lies in the mountainous tract south of the Caspian Sea; and it was from this mountain home he

obtained the evil celebrity among the Crusaders as the OLD MAN
OF THE MOUNTAINS, and spread terror through the Mohammedan world; and it is yet disputed whether the word *Assassin*,
which they have left in the language of modern Europe as their
dark memorial, is derived from the *hashish*, or opiate of hemp-
leaves (the Indian *bhang*), with which they maddened themselves to
the sullen pitch of oriental desperation, or from the name of the
founder of the dynasty, whom we have seen in his quiet collegiate
days, at Naishápúr. One of the countless victims of the Assassin's
dagger was Nizám-ul-Mulk himself, the old school-boy friend.[1]

"Omar Khayyám also came to the Vizier to claim his share; but
not to ask for title or office. 'The greatest boon you can confer on
me,' he said, 'is to let me live in a corner under the shadow of your
fortune, to spread wide the advantages of Science, and pray for
your long life and prosperity.' The Vizier tell us, that, when he
found Omar was really sincere in his refusal, he pressed him no
further, but granted him a yearly pension of 1200 *mithkáls* of gold,
from the treasury of Naishápúr.

"At Naishápúr thus lived and died Omar Khayyám, 'busied,'
adds the Vizier, 'in winning knowledge of every kind, and
especially in Astronomy, wherein he attained to a very high pre-
eminence. Under the Sultanate of Malik Shah, he came to Merv,
and obtained great praise for his proficiency in science, and the
Sultán showered favours upon him.'

"When Malik Shah determined to reform the calendar, Omar
was one of the eight learned men employed to do it; the result was
the *Jaláli* era (so called from *Jalál-ud-din*, one of the king's names) –
'a computation of time,' says Gibbon, 'which surpasses the Julian,
and approaches the accuracy of the Gregorian style.' He is also the
author of some astronomical tables, entitled Zíji-Maliksháhi," and

---

[1] Some of Omar's *Rubáiyát* warn us of the danger of Greatness, the instability of Fortune, and
while advocating Charity to all Men, recommending us to be too intimate with none. Attár
makes Nizám-ul-Mulk use the very words of his friend Omar [*Rub.* xxviii], "When Nizám-ul-
Mulk was in the Agony (of Death) he said, 'Oh God! I am passing away in the hand of the
wind.'"

the French have lately republished and translated an Arabic Treatise of his on Algebra.

"His Takhallus or poetical name (Khayyám) signifies a Tent-maker, and he is said to have at one time exercised that trade, perhaps before Nizám-ul-Mulk's generosity raised him to independence. Many Persian poets similarly derive their names from their occupations; thus we have Attár, 'a druggist,' Assár, 'an oil presser,' etc.[1] Omar himself alludes to his name in the following whimsical lines:

"'Khayyám, who stitched the tents of science,
    Has fallen in grief's furnace and been suddenly burned;
    The shears of Fate have cut the tent ropes of his life,
    And the broker of Hope has sold him for nothing!'

"We have only one more anecdote to give of his Life, and that relates to the close; it is told in the anonymous preface which is sometimes prefixed to his poems; it has been printed in the Persian in the Appendix to Hyde's *Veterum Persarum Religio*, p. 499; and D'Herbelot alludes to it in his Bibliothèque, under *Khiam*. – [2]

" 'It is written in the chronicles of the ancients that this King of the Wise, Omar Khayyám, died at Naishápúr in the year of the Hegira, 517 (A.D. 1123); in science he was unrivalled, – the very paragon of his age. Khwájah Nizámi of Samarcand, who was one of his pupils, relates the following story: "I often used to hold conversations with my teacher, Omar Khayyám, in a garden, and one day he said to me, 'My tomb shall be in a spot where the north wind may scatter roses over it.' I wondered at the words he spake, but I knew that his were no idle words.[3]

[1] Though all these, like our Smiths, Archers, Millers, Fletchers, etc., may simply retain the Surname of an hereditary calling.

[2] "*Philosophe Musulman qui a vecu en Odeur de Sainteté dans sa Religion, vers la Fin du premir et le Commencement du second Siècle*," no part of which, except the *Philosophe*, can apply to our Khayyám.

[3] The Rashness of the Words, according to D'Herbelot, consisted in being so opposed to those in the Korán: "No Man knows where he shall die." – This story of Omar reminds me of another

Years after, when I chanced to revisit Naishápúr, I went to his final resting-place, and lo! it was just outside a garden, and trees laden with fruit stretched their boughs over the garden wall, and dropped their flowers upon his tomb, so that the stone was hidden under them." ' "

Thus far – without fear of Trespass – from the *Calcutta Review*. The writer of it, on reading in India this story of Omar's Grave, was reminded, he said, of Cicero's Account of finding Archimedes' Tomb at Syracuse, buried in grass and weeds. I think Thorwaldsen desired to have roses grow over him; a wish religiously fulfilled for him to the present day, I believe. However, to return to Omar.

Though the Sultán "shower'd Favours upon him," Omar's Epicurean Audacity of Thought and Speech caused him to be regarded askance in his own Time and Country. He is said to have been especially hated and dreaded by the Sufis, whose Practice he ridiculed, and whose Faith amounted to little more than his own, when stript of the Mysticism and formal recognition of Islamism under which Omar would not hide. Their Poets, including Háfiz, who are (with the exception of Firdausi) the most considerable in Persia, borrowed largely, indeed, of Omar's material, but turning it to a mystical Use more convenient to Themselves and the People they addressed; a People quite as quick of Doubt as of Belief; as keen of Bodily Sense as of Intellectual; and delighting in a cloudy composition of both, in which they could float luxuriously between Heaven and Earth, and this World and the Next, on the wings of a poetical expression, that might serve indifferently for either. Omar was too honest of Heart as well as of Head for this.

so naturally – and when one remembers how wide of his humble mark the noble sailor aimed – so pathetically told by Captain Cook – not by Doctor Hawkesworth – in his Second Voyage (i. 374). When leaving Ulietea, "Oreo's last request was for me to return. When he saw he could not obtain that promise, he asked the name of my *Marai* (burying-place). As strange a question as this was, I hesitated not a moment to tell him 'Stepney;' the parish in which I live when in London. I was made to repeat it several times over till they could pronounce it; and then 'Stepney Marai no Toote' was echoed through an hundred mouths at once. I afterwards found the same question had been put to Mr. Forster by a man on shore; but he gave a different, and indeed more proper answer, by saying, 'No man who used the sea could say where he should be buried.'"

Having failed (however mistakenly) of finding any Providence but Destiny, and any World but This, he set about making the most of it; preferring rather to soothe the Soul through the Senses into Acquiescence with Things as he saw them, than to perplex it with vain disquietude after what they *might* be. It has been seen, however, that his Worldly Ambition was not exorbitant; and he very likely takes a humorous or perverse pleasure in exalting the gratification of Sense above that of the Intellect, in which he must have taken great delight, although it failed to answer the Questions in which he, in common with all men, was most vitally interested.

For whatever reason, however, Omar, as before said, has never been popular in his own Country, and therefore has been but scantily transmitted abroad. The MSS. of his Poems, mutilated beyond the average Casualties of Oriental Transcription, are so rare in the East as scarce to have reacht Westward at all, in spite of all the acquisitions of Arms and Science. There is no copy at the India House, none at the Bibliothèque Nationale of Paris. We know but of one in England: No. 140 of the Ouseley MSS. at the Bodleian, written at Shiráz, A.D. 1460. This contains but 158 *Rubáiyát.* One of the Asiatic Society's Library at Calcutta (of which we have a copy), contains (and yet incomplete). 516, though swelled to that by all kinds of Repetition and Corruption. So Von Hammer speaks of *his* Copy as containing about 200, while Dr. Sprenger catalogues the Lucknow MS. at double that number.[1] The Scribes, too, of the Oxford and Calcutta MSS. seem to do their Work under a sort of Protest; each beginning with a Tetrastich (whether genuine or not), taken out of its alphabetical order; the Oxford with one of Apology; the Calcutta with one of Expostulation, supposed (says a Notice prefixed to the MS.) to have arisen from a Dream, in which Omar's mother asked about his future fate. It may be rendered thus:

[1] "Since this paper was written" (adds the Reviewer in a note), "we have met with a Copy of a very rare Edition, printed at Calcutta in 1836. This contains 438 Tetrastichs, with an Appendix containing 54 others not found in some MSS."

" Oh, Thou who burn'st in Heart for those who burn
   In Hell, whose fires thyself shall feed in turn;
      How long be crying, 'Mercy on them, God!'
Why, who art Thou to teach, and He to learn?"

The Bodleian Quatrain pleads Pantheism by way of Justification.

" If I myself upon a looser Creed
   Have loosely strung the Jewel of Good deed,
   Let this one thing for my Atonement plead:
   That One for Two I never did mis-read."

The Reviewer,[1] to whom I owe the Particulars of Omar's Life, concludes his Review by comparing him with Lucretius, both as to natural Temper and Genius, and as acted upon by the Circumstances in which he lived. Both indeed were men of subtle, strong, and cultivated Intellect, fine Imagination, and Hearts passionate for Truth and Justice; who justly revolted from their Country's false Religion, and false, or foolish, Devotion to it; but who fell short of replacing what they subverted by such better *Hope* as others, with no better Revelation to guide them, had yet made a Law to themselves. Lucretius, indeed, with such material as Epicurus furnished, satisfied himself with the theory of a vast machine fortuitously constructed, and acting by a Law that implied no Legislator; and so composing himself into a Stoical rather than Epicurean severity of Attitude, sat down to contemplate the mechanical Drama of the Universe which he was part Actor in; himself and all about him (as in his own sublime description of the Roman Theatre) discoloured with the lurid reflex of the Curtain suspended between the Spectator and the Sun. Omar, more desperate, or more careless of any so complicated System as resulted in nothing but hopeless Necessity, flung his own Genius

[1] Professor Cowell.

and Learning with a bitter or humorous jest into the general Ruin which their insufficient glimpses only served to reveal; and, pretending sensual pleasure as the serious purpose of Life, only *diverted* himself with speculative problems of Deity, Destiny, Matter and Spirit, Good and Evil, and other such questions, easier to start than to run down, and the pursuit of which becomes a very weary spot at last!

With regard to the present Translation. The original *Rubáiyát* (as, missing an Arabic Guttural, these *Tetrastichs* are more musically called) are independent Stanzas, consisting each of four Lines of equal, though varied, Prosody; sometimes *all* rhyming, but oftener (as here imitated) the third line a blank. Somewhat as in the Greek Alcaic, where the penultimate line seems to lift and suspend the Wave that falls over in the last. As usual with such kind of Oriental Verse, the *Rubáiyát* follow one another according to Alphabetic Rhyme – a strange succession of Grave and Gay. Those here selected are strung into something of an Eclogue, with perhaps a less than equal proportion of the "Drink and make-merry," which (genuine or not), recurs over-frequently in the Original. Either way, the Result is sad enough: saddest perhaps when most ostentatiously merry: more apt to move Sorrow than Anger toward the old Tent-maker, who, after vainly endeavouring to unshackle his Steps from Destiny, and to catch some authentic Glimpse of TO-MORROW, fell back upon TO-DAY (which has outlasted so many To-morrows!) as the only Ground he had got to stand upon, however momentarily slipping from under his Feet.

## INTRODUCTION TO THIRD EDITION

WHILE the second Edition of this version of Omar was preparing, Monsieur Nicolas, French Consul at Resht, published a very careful and very good Edition of the Text, from a lithograph copy at Teheran, comprising 464 *Rubáiyát*, with translation and notes of his own.

Mons. Nicolas, whose Edition has reminded me of several things, and instructed me in others, does not consider Omar to be the material Epicurean that I have literally taken him for, but a Mystic, shadowing the Deity under the figure of Wine, Wine-bearer, &c., as Háfiz is supposed to do; in short, a Sufi poet like Háfiz and the rest.

I cannot see reason to alter my opinion, formed as it was more than a dozen years ago (1868) when Omar was first shown me by one to whom I am indebted for all I know of Oriental, and very much of other, literature. He admired Omar's Genius so much, that he would gladly have adopted any such Interpretation of his meaning as Mons. Nicolas' if he could.[1] That he could not, appears by his Paper in the *Calcutta Review* already so largely quoted; in which he argues from the Poems themselves, as well as from what records remain of the Poet's Life. And if more were needed to disprove Mons. Nicolas' Theory, there is the Biographical Notice which he himself has drawn up in direct contradiction to the Interpretation of the Poems given in his Notes. (See pp. xiii-xiv of his Preface.) Indeed I hardly knew poor Omar was so far gone till his Apologist informed me. For here we see that whatever were the Wine that Háfiz drank and sang, the veritable Juice of the Grape it was which Omar used, not only when carousing with his friends, but (says Mons. Nicolas) in order to excite himself to that pitch of

[1] Perhaps would have edited the Poems himself some years ago. He may now as little approve of my Version on one side, as of Mons. Nicholas' Theory on the other.

Devotion which others reached by cries and "*hurlemens.*" And yet, whenever Wine, Wine-bearer, &c., occur in the text – which is often enough – Mons. Nicolas carefully annotates "*Dieu,*" "*La Divinité,*" &c.: so carefully indeed that one is tempted to think that he was indoctrinated by the Sufi with whom he read the Poems. (Note to Rub. ii. p. 8.) A Persian would naturally wish to vindicate a distinguished Countryman; and a Sufi to enrol him in his own sect, which already comprises all the chief Poets of Persia.

What historical Authority has Mons. Nicolas to show that Omar gave himself up "*avec passion à l'étude de la philosophie des Soufis?*" (Preface, p. xiii.) The Doctrines of Pantheism, Materialism, Necessity, &c., were not peculiar to the Sufi; nor to Lucretius before them; nor to Epicurus before him; probably the very original Irreligion of Thinking men from the first; and very likely to be the spontaneous growth of a Philosopher living in an Age of social and political barbarism, under shadow of one of the Two and Seventy Religions supposed to divide the world. Von Hammer (according to Sprenger's Oriental Catalogue) speaks of Omar as "a Free-thinker, and *a great opponent of Sufism;*" perhaps because, while holding much of their Doctrine, he would not pretend to any inconsistent severity of morals. Sir W. Ouseley has written a note to something of the same effect on the fly-leaf of the Bodleian MS. And in two *Rubáiyát* of Mons. Nicolas' own Edition Suf and Sufi are both disparagingly named.

No doubt many of these Quatrains seem unaccountable unless mystically interpreted; but many more as unaccountable unless literally. Were the Wine spiritual, for instance, how wash the Body with it when dead? Why make cups of the dead clay to be filled with – "*La Divinité*" – by some succeeding Mystic? Mons. Nicolas himself is puzzled by some "*bizarres*" and "*trop Orientales*" allusions and images – "*d'une sensualité quelquefois révoltante*" indeed – which "*les convenances*" do not permit him to translate; but still which the reader cannot but refer to "*La Divinité.*"[1] No doubt also many of

[1] A Note to Quatrain 234 admits that, however clear the mystical meaning of such Images must be to Europeans, they are not quoted without "*rougissant*" even by laymen in Persia –

the Quatrains in the Teheran, as in the Calcutta, Copies, are spurious; such *Rubáiyát* being the common form of Epigram in Persia. But this, at best, tells as much one way as another; nay, the Sufi, who may be considered the Scholar and Man of Letters in Persia, would be far more likely than the careless Epicure to interpolate what favours his own view of the Poet. I observe that very few of the more mystical Quatrains are in the Bodleian MS. which must be one of the oldest, as dated at Shiraz, A.H. 865, A.D. 1460. And this, I think, especially distinguishes Omar (I cannot help calling him by his – no, not Christian – familiar name) from all other Persian Poets: That, whereas with them the Poet is lost in his Song, the Man in Allegory and Abstraction; we seem to have the Man – the *Bonhomme* – Omar himself, with all his Humours and Passions, as frankly before us as if we were really at Table with him, after the Wine had gone round. I must say that I, for one, never wholly believed in the Mysticism of Háfiz. It does not appear there was any danger in holding and singing Sufi Pantheism, so long as the Poet made his Salaam to Mohammed at the beginning and end of his Song. Under such conditions Jeláluddín, Jámi, Attár, and others sang; using Wine and Beauty indeed as Images to illustrate, not as a Mask to hide, the Divinity they were celebrating. Perhaps some Allegory less liable to mistake or abuse had been better among so inflammable a People: much more so when, as some think with Háfiz and Omar, the abstract is not only likened to, but identified with, the sensual Image; hazardous, if not to the Devotee himself, yet to his weaker Brethren; and worse for the Profane in proportion as the Devotion of the Initiated grew warmer. And all for what? To be tantalised with Images of sensual enjoyment which must be renounced if one would approximate a God, who according to the Doctrine, *is* Sensual Matter as well as Spirit, and

"*Quant aux termes de tendresse qui commencent ce quatrain, comme tant d'autres dans ce recueil, nos lecteurs, habitués maintenant à l'étrangeté des expressions si souvent employées par Khéyam pour rendre ses pensées sur l'amour divin, et à la singularité de ses images trop orientales, d'une sensualité quelquefois révoltante, n'auront pas de peine à se persuader qu'il s'agit de la Divinité, bien que cette conviction soit vivement discutée par les moullahs musulmans et même par beaucoup de laïques, qui rougissent véritablement d'une pareille licence de leur compatriote à l'égard des choses spirituelles.*"

into whose Universe one expects unconsciously to merge after Death, without hope of any posthumous Beatitude in another world to compensate for all one's self-denial in this. Lucretius' blind Divinity certainly merited, and probably got, as much self-sacrifice as this of the Sufi; and the burden of Omar's Song – if not "Let us eat" – is assuredly – "Let us drink for To-morrow we die!" And if Háfiz meant quite otherwise by a similar language, he surely miscalculated when he devoted his Life and Genius to so equivocal a Psalmody as, from his Day to this, has been said and sung by any rather than Spiritual Worshippers.

However, as there is some traditional presumption, and certainly the opinion of some learned men, in favour of Omar's being a Sufi – and even something of a Saint – those who please may so interpret his Wine and Cup-bearer. On the other hand, as there is far more historical certainty of his being a Philosopher, of scientific Insight and Ability far beyond that of the Age and Country he lived in; of such moderate worldly Ambition as becomes a Philosopher, and such moderate wants as rarely satisfy a De-bauchee; other readers may be content to believe with me that, while the Wine Omar celebrates is simply the Juice of the Grape, he bragged more than he drank of it, in very defiance perhaps of that Spiritual Wine which left its Votaries sunk in Hypocrisy or Disgust.

*Edward FitzGerald*

# THE FITZGERALD EDITIONS

*First Edition.*
RUBÁIYÁT OF OMAR KHAYYÁM, THE ASTRONOMER-POET OF PERSIA. Translated into English verse. London: Bernard Quaritch, Castle Street, Leicester Square. 1859.
*On the verso*: G. Norman, Printer, Maiden Lane, Covent Garden, London.
Small quarto. Brown paper wrappers, 75 quatrains, 22 notes.

*Second Edition.*
RUBÁIYÁT OF OMAR KHAYYÁM, THE ASTRONOMER-POET OF PERSIA. Rendered into English verse. Second Edition. London: Bernard Quaritch, Piccadilly. 1868.
(John Childs and Sons, Printers). Quarto. Paper wrappers, 110 quatrains, 25 notes.

*Third Edition.*
RUBÁIYÁT OF OMAR KHAYYÁM, the ASTRONOMER-POET OF PERSIA. Rendered into English verse. Third Edition. London: Bernard Quaritch, Piccadilly, 1872.
Quarto, half Roxburghe, maroon cloth. 101 quatrains.

*Fourth Edition.*
RUBÁIYÁT OF OMAR KHAYYÁM and the Salaman and Absal of Jami. Rendered into English verse. Bernard Quaritch, 15 Piccadilly, London. 1879.
F'cap, 4to, half Roxburghe, 101 quatrains.

*Fifth Edition.*
LETTERS AND LITERARY REMAINS OF EDWARD FITZGERALD, edited by William Aldis Wright, in Three Volumes. London: Macmillan and Co., and New York. 1889. *All Rights Reserved.*
Crown 8vo. Text in volume 3. 101 quatrains.

2nd September
1863

My dear and very dear Sir,
    I do not know in the least who are you, but I do with all
my soul pray you to find and translate some more of Omar
Khayyám for us: I never did – till this day – read anything so
glorious, to my mind as this poem – (10th. 11th. 12th pages
if one were to choose) – and that, and this, is all I can say
about it – More – more – please more – and that I am ever
gratefully and respectfully yours.

J. RUSKIN.

# RUBÁIYÁT OF OMAR KHAYYÁM

*The First Edition, 1859*

1

*AWAKE! for Morning in the Bowl of Night*

*Has flung the Stone that puts the Stars to Flight:*

*And Lo! the Hunter of the East has caught*

*The Sultán's Turret in a Noose of Light.*

2

*Dreaming when Dawn's Left Hand was in the Sky*

*I heard a voice within the Tavern cry,*

*"Awake, my Little ones, and fill the Cup*

*Before Life's Liquor in its Cup be dry."*

3

*And, as the Cock crew, those who stood before*

*The Tavern shouted — "Open then the Door!*

*You know how little while we have to stay,*

*And, once departed, may return no more."*

4

*Now the New Year reviving old Desires,*

*The thoughtful Soul to Solitude retires,*

*Where the W*HITE *H*AND OF *M*OSES *on the Bough*

*Puts out, and Jesus from the Ground suspires.*

5

*Iram indeed is gone with all its Rose,*

*And Jamshýd's Sev'n-ring'd Cup where no one knows;*

*But still the Vine her ancient ruby yields,*

*And still a Garden by the Water blows.*

6

*And David's Lips are lock't; but in divine*

*High piping Pehleví, with "Wine! Wine! Wine!*

*Red Wine!" – the Nightingale cries to the Rose*

*That yellow Cheek of her's to'incarnadine.*

7

Come, fill the Cup, and in the Fire of Spring

The Winter Garment of Repentance fling:

   The Bird of Time has but a little way

To fly — and Lo! the Bird is on the Wing.

8

And look — a thousand Blossoms with the Day

Woke — and a thousand scatter'd into Clay:

   And this first Summer Month that brings the Rose

Shall take Jamshýd and Kaikobád away.

9

But come with old Khayyám, and leave the Lot

Of Kaikobád and Kaikhosrú forgot:

  Let Rustum lay about him as he will,

Or Hátim Tai cry Supper — heed them not.


10

With me along some Strip of Herbage strown

That just divides the desert from the sown;

  Where name of Slave and Sultán scarce is known,

And pity Sultán Mahmud on his Throne.

11

*Here with a Loaf of Bread beneath the Bough,*

*A Flask of Wine, a Book of Verse — and Thou*

*Beside me singing in the Wilderness —*

*And Wilderness is Paradise enow.*

12

*"How sweet is mortal Sovranty!" — think some:*

*Others — "How blest the Paradise to come!"*

*Ah, take the Cash in hand and waive the Rest;*

*Oh, the brave Music of a distant Drum!*

13

*Look to the Rose that blows about us — "Lo,*

*Laughing," she says, "into the World I blow:*

*At once the silken Tassel of my Purse*

*Tear, and its Treasure on the Garden throw."*

14

*The Worldly Hope men set their Hearts upon*

*Turns Ashes — or it prospers; and anon,*

*Like Snow upon the Desert's dusty Face*

*Lightning a little Hour or two — is gone.*

15

And those who husbanded the Golden Grain,

And those who flung it to the Winds like Rain,

Alike to no such aureate Earth are turn'd

As, buried once, Men want dug up again.

16

Think, in this batter'd Caravanserai

Whose Doorways are alternate Night and Day,

How Sultán after Sultán with his Pomp

Abode his Hour or two and went his way.

17

*They say the Lion and the Lizard keep*

*The Courts where Jamshýd gloried and drank deep:*

*And Bahrám, that great Hunter — the Wild Ass*

*Stamps o'er his Head, and he lies fast asleep.*

18

*I sometimes think that never blows so red*

*The Rose as where some buried Cæsar bled;*

*That every Hyacinth the Garden wears*

*Dropt in its Lap from some once lovely Head.*

19

*And this delightful Herb whose tender Green*

*Fledges the River's Lip on which we lean –*

*Ah, lean upon it lightly! for who knows*

*From what once lovely Lip it springs unseen!*

20

*Ah, my Belovéd, fill the Cup that clears*

*To-day of past Regrets and future Fears –*

*To-morrow? – Why, To-morrow I may be*

*Myself with Yesterday's Sev'n Thousand Years.*

21

*Lo! some we loved, the lovliest and best*

*That Time and Fate of all their Vintage prest,*

*Have drunk their Cup a Round or two before,*

*And one by one crept silently to Rest.*

22

*And we, that now make merry in the Room*

*They left, and Summer dresses in new Bloom,*

*Ourselves must we beneath the Couch of Earth*

*Descend, ourselves to make a Couch — for whom?*

23

*Ah, make the most of what we yet may spend,*

*Before we too into the Dust descend;*

*Dust into Dust, and under Dust, to lie,*

*Sans Wine, sans Song, sans Singer, and — sans End*

24

*Alike for those who for* To-DAY *prepare,*

*And those that after a* To-MORROW *stare,*

*A Muezzin from the Tower of Darkness cries*

*"Fools! your Reward is neither Here nor There!"*

25

*Why, all the Saints and Sages who discuss'd*

*Of the Two Worlds so learnedly, are thrust*

*Like foolish Prophets forth; their Words to Scorn*

*Are scatter'd, and their Mouths are stopt with Dust.*

26

*Oh, come with old Khayyám, and leave the Wise*

*To talk; one thing is certain, that Life flies;*

*One thing is certain, and the Rest is Lies;*

*The Flower that once has blown for ever dies.*

O.K.            E

27

*Myself when young did eagerly frequent*

*Doctor and Saint, and heard great Argument*

  *About it and about; but evermore*

*Came out by the same Door as in I went.*

28

*With them the Seed of Wisdom did I sow,*

*And with my own hand labour'd it to grow:*

  *And this was all the Harvest that I reap'd —*

*"I came like Water and like Wind I go."*

29

*Into this Universe, and* why *not knowing,*

*Nor* whence, *like Water willy-nilly flowing:*

*And out of it, as Wind along the Waste,*

*I know not* whither, *willy-nilly blowing.*

30

*What, without asking, hither hurried* whence?

*And, without asking,* whither *hurried hence!*

*Another and another Cup to drown*

*The Memory of this Impertinence!*

31

Up from Earth's Centre through the Seventh Gate

I rose, and on the Throne of Saturn sate,

And many Knots unravel'd by the Road;

But not the Knot of Human Death and Fate.

32

There was a Door to which I found no Key:

There was a Veil past which I could not see:

Some little Talk awhile of M<small>E</small> and T<small>HEE</small>

There seemed — and then no more of T<small>HEE</small> and M<small>E</small>.

33

*Then to the rolling Heav'n itself I cried,*

*Asking, "What Lamp had Destiny to guide*

  *Her little Children stumbling in the Dark?"*

*And — "A blind Understanding!" Heav'n replied.*

34

*Then to this earthen Bowl did I adjourn*

*My Lip the secret Well of Life to learn:*

  *And Lip to Lip it murmur'd — "While you live*

*Drink! — for once dead you never shall return."*

35

*I think the Vessel, that with fugitive*

*Articulation answer'd, once did live,*

  *And merry-make; and the cold Lip I kiss'd*

*How many Kisses might it take — and give!*

36

*For in the Market-place, one Dusk of Day,*

*I watch'd the Potter thumping his wet Clay:*

  *And with its all obliterated Tongue*

*It murmur'd — "Gently, Brother, gently, pray!"*

## 37

*Ah, fill the Cup: — what boots it to repeat*

*How Time is slipping underneath our Feet:*

*Unborn, To-morrow, and dead Yesterday,*

*Why fret about them if To-day be sweet!*

## 38

*One Moment in Annihilation's Waste,*

*One Moment, of the Well of Life to taste —*

*The Stars are setting and the Caravan*

*Starts for the Dawn of Nothing — Oh, make haste!*

39

*How long, how long, in infinite Pursuit*

*Of This and That endeavour and dispute?*

*Better be merry with the fruitful Grape*

*Than sadden after none, or bitter, Fruit.*

40

*You know, my Friends, how long since in my Hous*

*For a new Marriage I did make Carouse:*

*Divorced old barren Reason from my Bed,*

*And took the Daughter of the Vine to Spouse.*

41

For "I*s*" and "I*s-not*" though with *Rule and Line*,

And "U*p-and-down*" without *I could define*,

I yet in all I only cared to know,

Was never deep in anything but — Wine.

42

And lately, by the Tavern Door agape,

Came stealing through the Dusk an Angel Shape

Bearing a Vessel on his Shoulder; and

He bid me taste of it; and 'twas — the Grape!

43

*The Grape that can with Logic absolute*

*The Two-and-Seventy jarring Sects confute:*

*The subtle Alchemist that in a Trice*

*Life's leaden Metal into Gold transmute.*

44

*The mighty Mahmud, the victorious Lord,*

*That all the misbelieving and black Horde*

*Of Fears and Sorrows that infest the Soul*

*Scatters and slays with his enchanted Sword.*

45

But leave the Wise to wrangle, and with me

The Quarrel of the Universe let be:

  And, in some corner of the Hubbub coucht,

Make Game of that which makes as much of Thee.

46

For in and out, above, about, below,

'Tis nothing but a Magic Shadow-show,

  Play'd in a Box whose Candle is the Sun,

Round which we Phantom Figures come and go.

47

*And if the Wine you drink, the Lip you press,*

*End in the Nothing all Things end in – Yes –*

*Then fancy while Thou art, Thou art but what*

*Thou shalt be – Nothing – Thou shalt not be less.*

48

*While the Rose blows along the River Brink,*

*With old Khayyám and Ruby Vintage drink:*

*And when the Angel with his darker Draught*

*Draws up to Thee – take that, and do not shrink.*

49

*'Tis all a Chequer-board of Nights and Days*

*Where Destiny with Men for Pieces plays:*

*Hither and thither moves, and mates, and slays,*

*And one by one back in the Closet lays.*

50

*The Ball no Question makes of Ayes and Noes,*

*But Right or Left, as strikes the Player goes;*

*And He that toss'd Thee down into the Field,*

*He knows about it all — HE knows — HE knows!*

51

*The Moving Finger writes; and, having writ,*

*Moves on: nor all thy Piety nor Wit*

*Shall lure it back to cancel half a Line,*

*Nor all thy Tears wash out a Word of it.*

52

*And that inverted Bowl we call The Sky,*

*Whereunder crawling coop't we live and die,*

*Lift not thy hands to It for help — for It*

*Rolls impotently on as Thou or I.*

### 53

*With Earth's first Clay They did the Last Man's knead*

*And then of the Last Harvest sow'd the Seed:*

*Yea, the first Morning of Creation wrote*

*What the Last Dawn of Reckoning shall read.*

### 54

*I tell Thee this — When, starting from the Goal,*

*Over the shoulders of the flaming Foal*

*Of Heav'n Parwín and Mushtara they flung,*

*In my predestin'd Plot of Dust and Soul.*

55

The Vine had struck a Fibre; which about

If clings my Being – let the Sufi flout;

  Of my Base Metal may be filed a Key,

That shall unlock the Door he howls without.

56

And this I know: whether the one True Light,

Kindle to Love, or Wrath – consume me quite,

  .One Glimpse of It within the Tavern caught

Better than in the Temple lost outright.

57

*Oh, Thou, who didst with Pitfall and with Gin*

*Beset the Road I was to wander in,*

*Thou wilt not with Predestination round*

*Enmesh me, and impute my Fall to Sin?*

58

*Oh, Thou, who Man of baser Earth didst make,*

*And who with Eden didst devise the Snake;*

*For all the Sin wherewith the Face of Man*

*Is blacken'd, Man's Forgiveness give — and take!*

O.K.                                                F

## *Kuza-Nama*

### 59

*Listen again. One Evening at the Close*

*Of Ramazán, ere the better Moon arose,*

*In that old Potter's Shop I stood alone*

*With the clay Population round in Rows.*

### 60

*And, strange to tell, among that Earthen Lot*

*Some could articulate, while others not:*

*And suddenly one more impatient cried —*

*"Who is the Potter, pray, and who the Pot?"*

### 61

*Then said another – "Surely not in vain*

*My Substance from the common Earth was ta'en,*

*That He who subtly wrought me into Shape*

*Should stamp me back to common Earth again."*

### 62

*Another said – "Why, ne'er a peevish Boy,*

*Would break the Bowl from which he drank in Joy;*

*Shall He that made the Vessel in pure Love*

*And Fancy, in an after Rage destroy!"*

63

None answer'd this; but after Silence spake

A Vessel of a more ungainly Make:

"They sneer at me for leaning all awry;

What! did the Hand then of the Potter shake?"

64

Said one — "Folks of a surly Tapster tell,

And daub his Visage with the Smoke of Hell;

They talk of some strict Testing of us — Pish!

He's a Good Fellow, and 'twill all be well."

65

*Then said another with a long-drawn Sigh,*

*"My Clay with long oblivion is gone dry:*

*But, fill me with the old familiar Juice,*

*Methinks I might recover by-and-bye!"*

66

*So while the Vessels one by one were speaking,*

*One spied the little Crescent all were seeking:*

*And then they jogg'd each other, "Brother! Brother!*

*Hark to the Porter's Shoulder-knot a-creaking!"*

67

*Ah, with the Grape my fading Life provide,*

*And wash my Body whence the Life has died,*

*And in a Windingsheet of Vine-leaf wrapt,*

*So bury me by some sweet Garden-side.*

68

*That ev'n my buried Ashes such a Snare*

*Of Perfume shall fling up into the Air,*

*As not a True Believer passing by*

*But shall be overtaken unaware.*

69

*Indeed the Idols I have loved so long*

*Have done my Credit in Men's Eye much wrong:*

  *Have drown'd my Honour in a shallow Cup,*

*And sold my Reputation for a Song.*

70

*Indeed, indeed, Repentance oft before*

*I swore — but was I sober when I swore?*

  *And then and then came Spring, and Rose-in-hand*

*My thread-bare Penitence apieces tore.*

71

And much as Wine has play'd the Infidel,

And robb'd me of my Robe of Honour – well,

  I often wonder what the Vintners buy

One half so precious as the Goods they sell.

72

Alas, that Spring should vanish with the Rose!

That Youth's sweet-scented Manuscript should close!

  The Nightingale that in the Branches sang,

Ah, whence, and whither flown again, who knows!

## 73

*Ah Love! could thou and I with Fate conspire*

*To grasp this sorry Scheme of Things entire,*

*Would not we shatter it to bits — and then*

*Re-mould it nearer to the Heart's Desire!*

## 74

*Ah, Moon of my Delight who know'st no wane,*

*The Moon of Heav'n is rising once again:*

*How oft hereafter rising shall she look*

*Through this same Garden after me — in vain!*

75

*And when Thyself with shining Foot shall pass*

*Among the Guests Star-scatter'd on the Grass,*

*And in thy joyous Errand reach the Spot*

*Where I made one – turn down an empty Glass!*

TAMÁM  SHUD

# RUBÁIYÁT OF OMAR KHAYYÁM

*The Second Edition*, 1868

I

*WAKE! For the Sun behind yon Eastern height*

*Has chased the Session of the Stars from Night;*

*And, to the field of Heav'n ascending, strikes*

*The Sultán's Turret with a Shaft of Light.*

2

*Before the phantom of False morning died,*

*Methought a Voice within the Tavern cried,*

*"When all the Temple is prepared within,*

*Why lags the drowsy Worshipper outside?"*

3

*And, as the Cock crew, those who stood before*

*The Tavern shouted – "Open then the door!*

*You know how little while we have to stay,*

*And, once departed, may return no more."*

4

*Now the New Year reviving old Desires,*

*The thoughtful Soul to Solitude retires,*

*Where the WHITE HAND OF MOSES on the Bough*

*Puts out, and Jesus from the ground suspires.*

5

Iram indeed is gone with all his Rose,

And Jamshýd's Sev'n-ring'd Cup where no one knows;

  But still a Ruby gushes from the Vine,

And many a Garden by the Water blows.

6

And David's lips are lockt; but in divine

High-piping Pehleví, with "Wine! Wine! Wine!

  Red Wine!" – the Nightingale cries to the Rose

That sallow cheek of her's to incarnadine.

7

*Come, fill the Cup, and in the fire of Spring*

*Your Winter-garment of Repentance fling:*

*The Bird of Time has but a little way*

*To flutter – and the Bird is on the Wing.*

8

*Whether at Naishápúr or Babylon,*

*Whether the Cup with sweet or bitter run,*

*The Wine of Life keeps oozing drop by drop,*

*The Leaves of Life keep falling one by one.*

9

*Morning a thousand Roses brings, you say;*

*Yes, but where leaves the Rose of yesterday?*

*And this first Summer month that brings the Rose*

*Shall take Jamshýd and Kaikobád away.*

10

*Well, let it take them! What have we to do*

*With Kaikobád the Great, or Kaikhosrú?*

*Let Rustum cry "To Battle!" as he likes,*

*Or Hátim Tai "To Supper!" — heed not you.*

11

*With me along the strip of Herbage strown*

*That just divides the desert from the sown,*

*Where name of Slave and Sultán is forgot —*

*And Peace to Mahmud on his golden Throne!*

12

*Here with a little Bread beneath the Bough,*

*A Flask of Wine, a Book of Verse — and Thou*

*Beside me singing in the Wilderness —*

*Oh, Wilderness were Paradise enow!*

13

*Some for the Glories of This World; and some*

*Sigh for the Prophet's Paradise to come;*

*Ah, take the Cash, and let the Promise go,*

*Nor heed the rumble of a distant Drum!*

14

*Were it not Folly, Spider-like to spin*

*The Thread of present Life away to win —*

*What? for ourselves, who know not if we shall*

*Breathe out the very Breath we now breathe in!*

15

*Look to the blowing Rose about us – "Lo,*

*Laughing," she says, "into the world I blow:*

*At once the silken tassel of my Purse*

*Tear, and its Treasure on the Garden throw."*

16

*For those who husbanded the Golden grain,*

*And those who flung it to the winds like Rain,*

*Alike to no such aureate Earth are turn'd*

*As, buried once, Men want dug up again.*

## 17

*The Worldly Hope men set their Hearts upon*

*Turns Ashes — or it prospers; and anon,*

*  Like Snow upon the Desert's dusty Face,*

*Lighting a little hour or two — was gone.*

## 18

*Think, in this batter'd Caravanserai*

*Whose Portals are alternate Night and Day,*

*  How Sultán after Sultán with his Pomp*

*Abode his destin'd Hour, and went his way.*

19

They say the Lion and the Lizard keep

The Courts where Jamshýd gloried and drank deep:

And Bahrám, that great Hunter – the Wild Ass

Stamps o'er his Head, but cannot break his Sleep.

20

The Palace that to Heav'n his pillars threw,

And Kings the forehead on his threshold drew –

I saw the solitary Ringdove there,

And "Coo, coo, coo," she cried; "Coo, coo, coo."

21

*Ah, my Belovéd, fill the Cup that clears*

*T*O-DAY *of past Regrets and future Fears:*

  *To-morrow! – Why, To-morrow I may be*

*Myself with Yesterday's Sev'n thousand Years.*

22

*For some we loved, the loveliest and the best*

*That from his Vintage rolling Time has prest,*

  *Have drunk their Cup a Round or two before,*

*And one by one crept silently to rest.*

23

And we, that now make merry in the Room

They left, and Summer dresses in new bloom,

 Ourselves must we beneath the Couch of Earth

Descend, ourselves to make a Couch — for whom?

24

I sometimes think that never blows so red

The Rose as where some buried Cæsar bled;

 That every Hyacinth the Garden wears

Dropt in her Lap from some once lovely Head.

25

And this delightful Herb whose living Green

Fledges the River's Lip on which we lean —

Ah, lean upon it lightly! for who knows

From what once lovely Lip it springs unseen!

26

Ah, make the most of what we yet may spend,

Before we too into the Dust descend;

Dust into Dust, and under Dust, to lie,

Sans Wine, sans Song, sans Singer, and — sans End!

27

*Alike for those who for T*O-DAY *prepare,*

*And those that after some T*O-MORROW *stare,*

*A Muezzin from the Tower of Darkness cries,*

*"Fools! your Reward is neither Here nor There!"*

28

*Another Voice, when I am sleeping, cries,*

*"The Flower should open with the Morning skies."*

*And a retreating Whisper, as I wake —*

*"The Flower that once has blown for ever dies."*

29

*Why, all the Saints and Sages who discuss'd*

*Of the Two Worlds so learnedly, are thrust*

*Like foolish Prophets forth; their Words to Scorn*

*Are scatter'd, and their Mouths are stopt with Dust.*

30

*Myself when young did eagerly frequent*

*Doctor and Saint, and heard great argument*

*About it and about: but evermore*

*Came out by the same door as in I went.*

31

With them the seed of Wisdom did I sow,

And with mine own hand wrought to make it grow:

And this was all the Harvest that I reap'd —

"I came like Water, and like Wind I go."

32

Into this Universe, and Why not knowing,

Nor Whence, like Water willy-nilly flowing:

And out of it, as Wind along the Waste,

I know not Whither, willy-nilly blowing.

### 33

*What, without asking, hither hurried* Whence?

*And, without asking,* Whither *hurried hence!*

*Ah, contrite Heav'n endowed us with the Vine*

*To drug the memory of that insolence!*

### 34

*Up from Earth's Centre through the Seventh Gate*

*I rose, and on the Throne of Saturn sate,*

*And many Knots unravel'd by the Road;*

*But not the Master-Knot of Human Fate.*

35

There was the Door to which I found no Key:

There was the Veil through which I could not see

Some little talk awhile of M*E* and T*HEE*

There was — and then no more of T*HEE* and M*E*.

36

Earth could not answer; nor the Seas that mourn

In flowing Purple, of their Lord forlorn;

Nor Heav'n, with those eternal Signs reveal'd

And hidden by the sleeve of Night and Morn.

## 37

*Then of the T*HEE IN *M*E *who works behind*

*The Veil of Universe I cried to find*

 *A Lamp to guide me through the Darkness; and*

*Something then said – "An Understanding blind."*

## 38

*Then to the Lip of this poor earthen Urn*

*I lean'd, the secret Well of Life to learn:*

 *And Lip to Lip it murmur'd – "While you live,*

*Drink! – for, once dead, you never shall return."*

39

*I think the Vessel, that with fugitive*

*Articulation answer'd, once did live,*

  *And drink; and that impassive Lip I kiss'd,*

*How many Kisses might it take – and give!*

40

*For I remember stopping by the way*

*To watch a Potter thumping his wet Clay:*

  *And with its all-obliterated Tongue*

*It murmur'd – "Gently, Brother, gently, pray!"*

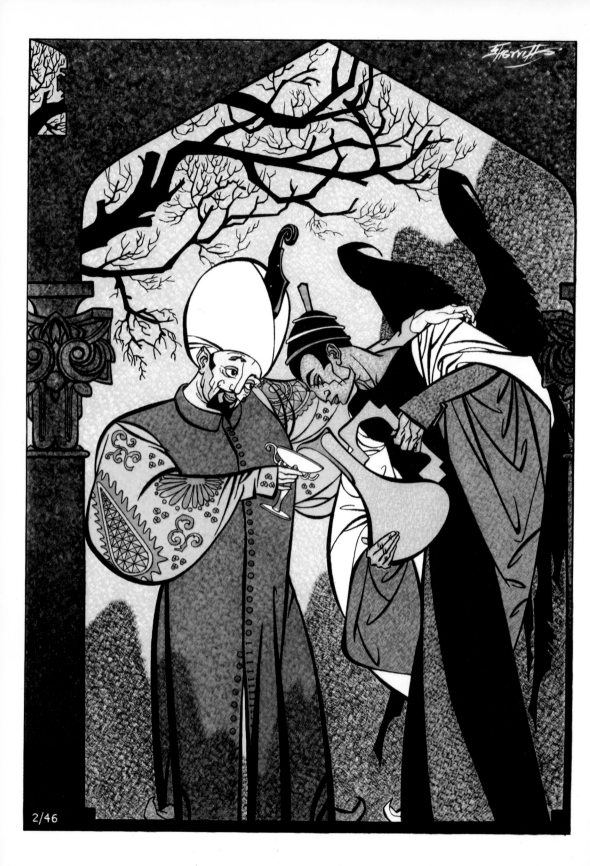

41

*For has not such a Story from of Old*

*Down Man's successive generations roll'd*

*Of such a clod of saturated Earth*

*Cast by the Maker into Human mould?*

42

*And not a drop that from our Cups we throw*

*On the parcht herbage but may steal below*

*To quench the fire of Anguish in some Eye*

*There hidden — far beneath, and long ago.*

O.K.

H

43

As then the Tulip for her wonted sup

Of Heavenly Vintage lifts her chalice up,

  Do you, twin offspring of the soil, till Heav'n

To Earth invert you like an empty Cup.

44

Do you, within your little hour of Grace,

The waving Cypress in your Arms enlace,

  Before the Mother back into her arms

Fold, and dissolve you in a last embrace.

45

*And if the Cup you drink, the Lip you press,*

*End in what All begins and ends in — Yes;*

*Imagine then you are what heretofore*

*You were — hereafter you shall not be less.*

46

*So when at last the Angel of the darker drink*

*Of Darkness finds you by the river-brink,*

*And, proffering his Cup, invites your Soul*

*Forth to your Lips to quaff it — do not shrink.*

47

*And fear not lest Existence closing your*

*Account, should lose, or know the type no more;*

*The Eternal Sákí from that Bowl has pour'd*

*Millions of Bubbles like us, and will pour.*

48

*When You and I behind the Veil are past,*

*Oh but the long long while the World shall last,*

*Which of our Coming and Departure heeds*

*As much as Ocean of a pebble-cast.*

49

*One Moment in Annihilation's Waste,*

*One Moment, of the Well of Life to taste —*

*The Stars are setting, and the Caravan*

*Draws to the Dawn of Nothing — Oh make haste!*

50

*Would you that spangle of Existence spend*

*About* THE SECRET *— quick about it, Friend!*

*A Hair, they say, divides the False and True —*

*And upon what, prithee, does Life depend?*

51

*A Hair, they say, divides the False and True;*

*Yes; and a single Alif were the clue,*

  *Could you but find it, to the Treasure-house,*

*And peradventure to T*HE *M*ASTER *too;*

52

*Whose secret Presence, through Creation's veins*

*Running, Quicksilver-like eludes your pains:*

  *Taking all shapes from Máh to Máhi; and*

*They change and perish all — but He remains;*

### 53

*A moment guess'd — then back behind the Fold*

*Immerst of Darkness round the Drama roll'd*

*Which, for the Pastime of Eternity,*

*He doth Himself contrive, enact, behold.*

### 54

*But if in vain, down on the stubborn floor*

*Of Earth, and up to Heav'n's unopening Door,*

*You gaze To-day, while You are You — how then*

*To-morrow, You when shall be You no more?*

55

*Of, plagued no more with Human or Divine,*

*To-morrow's tangle to itself resign,*

*And lose your fingers in the tresses of*

*The Cypress-slender Minister of Wine.*

56

*Waste not your Hour, nor in the vain pursuit*

*Of This and That endeavour and dispute;*

*Better be merry with the fruitful Grape*

*Than sadden after none, or bitter, Fruit.*

57

*You know, my Friends, how bravely in my House*

*For a new Marriage I did make Carouse:*

*Divorced old barren Reason from my Bed,*

*And took the Daughter of the Vine to Spouse.*

58

*For "Is" and "Is-not" though with Rule and Line,*

*And "Up-and-down" by Logic I define,*

*Of all that one should care to fathom, I*

*Was never deep in anything but — Wine.*

59

*Ah, but my Computations, People say,*

*Have squared the Year to human compass, eh?*

*If so, by striking from the Calendar*

*Unborn To-morrow, and dead Yesterday.*

60

*And lately, by the Tavern Door agape,*

*Came shining through the Dusk an Angel Shape*

*Bearing a Vessel on his Shoulder; and*

*He bid me taste of it; and 'twas — the Grape!*

61

*The Grape that can with Logic absolute*

*The Two-and-Seventy jarring Sects confute:*

*The sovereign Alchemist that in a trice*

*Life's leaden metal into Gold transmute:*

62

*The mighty Mahmud, Allah-breathing Lord,*

*That all the misbelieving and black Horde*

*Of Fears and Sorrows that infest the Soul*

*Scatters before him with his whirlwind Sword.*

63

*Why, be this Juice the growth of God, who dare*

*Blaspheme the twisted tendril as a Snare?*

  *A Blessing, we should use it, should we not?*

*And if a Curse – why, then, Who set it there?*

64

*I must abjure the Balm of Life, I must,*

*Scared by some After-reckoning ta'en on trust,*

  *Or lured with Hope of some Diviner Drink,*

*When the frail Cup is crumbled into Dust!*

65

*If but the Vine and Love-abjuring Band*

*Are in the Prophet's Paradise to stand,*

*Alack, I doubt the Prophet's Paradise*

*Were empty as the hollow of one's Hand.*

66

*Oh threats of Hell and Hopes of Paradise!*

*One thing at least is certain — This Life flies:*

*One thing is certain and the rest is lies;*

*The Flower that once is blown for ever dies.*

## 67

Strange, is it not? that of the myriads who

Before us pass'd the door of Darkness through

Not one returns to tell us of the Road,

Which to discover we must travel too.

## 68

The Revelations of Devout and Learn'd

Who rose before us, and as Prophets burn'd,

Are all but Stories, which, awoke from Sleep

They told their fellows, and to Sleep return'd.

69

*Why, if the Soul can fling the Dust aside,*

*And naked on the Air of Heaven ride,*

*Is't not a shame — is't not a shame for him*

*So long in this Clay suburb to abide?*

70

*But that is but a Tent wherein may rest*

*A Sultán to the realm of Death addrest;*

*The Sultán rises, and the dark Ferrásh*

*Strikes, and prepares it for another guest.*

71

I sent my Soul through the Invisible,

Some letter of that After-life to spell:

  And after many days my Soul return'd

And said, "Behold, Myself am Heav'n and Hell:"

72

Heav'n but the Vision of fulfill'd Desire,

And Hell the Shadow of a Soul on fire,

  Cast on the Darkness into which Ourselves,

So late emerg'd from, shall so soon expire.

### 73

*We are no other than a moving row*

*Of visionary Shapes that come and go*

*Round with this Sun-illumin'd Lantern held*

*In Midnight by the Master of the Show;*

### 74

*Impotent Pieces of the Game he plays*

*Upon this Chequer-board of Nights and Days;*

*Hither and thither moves, and checks, and slays;*

*And one by one back in the Closet lays.*

75

*The Ball no Question makes of Ayes and Noes,*

*But Right or Left as strikes the Player goes;*

*And He that toss'd you down into the Field,*

He *knows about it all —* HE *knows —* HE *knows!*

76

*The Moving Finger writes; and, having writ,*

*Moves on: nor all your Piety nor Wit*

*Shall lure it back to cancel half a Line,*

*Nor all your Tears wash out a Word of it.*

77

*For let Philosopher and Doctor preach*

*Of what they will, and what they will not — each*

*Is but one Link in an eternal Chain*

*That none can slip, nor break, nor over-reach.*

78

*And that inverted Bowl we call The Sky,*

*Whereunder crawling coop'd we live and die,*

*Lift not your hands to It for help — for It*

*As impotently rolls as you or I.*

79

*With Earth's first Clay They did the Last Man kne*

*And there of the Last Harvest sow'd the Seed;*

*And the first Morning of Creation wrote*

*What the Last Dawn of Reckoning shall read.*

80

*Yesterday This Day's Madness did prepare;*

*To-morrow's Silence, Triumph, or Despair:*

*Drink! for know you not whence you came, nor wl*

*Drink! for you know not why you go, nor where.*

81

*I tell you this — When, started from the Goal,*

*Over the flaming shoulders of the Foal*

  *Of Heav'n Parwín and Mushtari they flung,*

*In my predestin'd Plot of Dust and Soul*

82

*The Vine had struck a fibre: which about*

*If clings my Being — let the Dervish flout;*

  *Of my Base metal may be filed a Key,*

*That shall unlock the Door he howls without.*

83

*And this I know: whether the one True Light,*

*Kindle to Love, or Wrath-consume me quite,*

*One Flash of It within the Tavern caught*

*Better than in the Temple lost outright.*

84

*What! out of senseless Nothing to provoke*

*A conscious Something to resent the yoke*

*Of unpermitted Pleasure, under pain*

*Of Everlasting Penalties, if broke!*

85

*What! from his helpless Creature be repaid*

*Pure Gold for what he lent us dross-allay'd —*

*Sue for a Debt we never did contract,*

*And cannot answer — Oh the sorry trade!*

86

*Nay, but, for terror of his wrathful Face,*

*I swear I will not call Injustice Grace;*

*Not one Good Fellow of the Tavern but*

*Would kick so poor a Coward from the place.*

87

*Oh Thou, who didst with pitfall and with gin*

*Beset the Road I was to wander in,*

  *Thou wilt not with Predestin'd Evil round*

*Enmesh, and then impute my Fall to Sin?*

88

*Oh Thou, who Man of baser Earth didst make,*

*And ev'n with Paradise devise the Snake:*

  *For all the sin the Face of wretched Man*

*Is black with — Man's Forgiveness give — and take!*

89

*As under cover of departing Day*

*Slunk hunger-stricken Ramazán away,*

*Once more within the Potter's house alone*

*I stood, surrounded by the Shapes of Clay.*

90

*And once again there gather'd a scarce heard*

*Whisper among them; as it were, the stirr'd*

*Ashes of some all but extinguisht Tongue,*

*Which mine ear kindled into living Word.*

91

Said one among them — "Surely not in vain,

My Substance from the common Earth was ta'en,

That He who subtly wrought me into Shape

Should stamp me back to shapeless Earth again?"

92

Another said, "Why, ne'er a peevish Boy

Would break the Cup from which he drank in Joy;

Shall He that of his own free Fancy made

The Vessel, in an after-rage destroy!"

93

None answer'd this; but after silence spake

Some Vessel of a more ungainly Make;

"They sneer at me for leaning all awry;

What! did the Hand then of the Potter shake?"

94

Thus with the Dead as with the Living, What?

And Why? so ready, but the Wherefor not,

One on a sudden peevishly exclaim'd,

"Which is the Potter, pray, and which the Pot?"

### 95

Said one – "Folks of a surly Master tell,

And daub his Visage with the Smoke of Hell;

They talk of some sharp Trial of us – Pish!

He's a Good Fellow, and 'twill all be well."

### 96

"Well," said another, "Whoso will, let try,

My Clay with long oblivion is gone dry:

But, fill me with the old familiar Juice,

Methinks I might recover by-and-bye!"

### 97

*So while the Vessels one by one were speaking,*

*One spied the little Crescent all were seeking:*

  *And then they jogg'd each other, "Brother! Brother!*

*Now for the Porter's shoulder-knot a-creaking!"*

★    ★    ★    ★    ★

### 98

*Ah, with the Grape my fading Life provide,*

*And wash my Body whence the Life has died,*

  *And lay me, shrouded in the living Leaf,*

*By some not unfrequented Garden-side.*

99

Whither resorting from the vernal Heat

Shall Old Acquaintance Old Acquaintance greet,

Under the Branch that leans above the Wall

To shed his Blossom over head and feet.

100

Then ev'n my buried Ashes such a snare

Of Vintage shall fling up into the Air,

As not a True-believer passing by

But shall be overtaken unaware.

101

*Indeed the Idols I have loved so long*

*Have done my credit in Men's eye much wrong:*

*Have drown'd my Glory in a shallow Cup,*

*And sold my Reputation for a Song.*

102

*Indeed, indeed, Repentance oft before*

*I swore — but was I sober when I swore?*

*And then and then came Spring and Rose-in-hand*

*My thread-bare Penitence apieces tore.*

103

And much as Wine has play'd the Infidel,

And robb'd me of my Robe of Honour – Well,

  I often wonder what the Vintners buy

One half so precious as the ware they sell.

104

Yet Ah, that Spring should vanish with the Rose!

That Youth's sweet-scented manuscript should close!

  The Nightingale that in the branches sang,

Ah whence, and whither flown again, who knows!

2/73

105

*Would but the Desert of the Fountain yield*

*One glimpse – if dimly, yet indeed, reveal'd,*

*Toward which the fainting Traveller might spring,*

*As springs the trampled herbage of the field!*

106

*Oh if the World were but to re-create,*

*That we might catch ere closed the Book of Fate,*

*And make The Writer on a fairer leaf*

*Inscribe our names, or quite obliterate!*

O.K.                                                    K

107

Better, oh better, cancel from the Scroll

Of Universe one luckless Human Soul,

   Than drop by drop enlarge the Flood that rolls

Hoarser with Anguish as the Ages roll.

108

Ah Love! could you and I with Fate conspire

To grasp this sorry Scheme of Things entire,

   Would not we shatter it to bits — and then

Re-mould it nearer to the Heart's Desire!

109

But see! The rising Moon of Heav'n again

Looks for us, Sweet-heart, through the quivering Plane:

How oft hereafter rising will she look

Among those leaves — for one of us in vain!

110

And when Yourself with silver Foot shall pass

Among the Guests Star-scatter'd on the Grass,

And in your joyous errand reach the spot

Where I made One — turn down an empty Glass!

TAMÁM

# RUBÁIYÁT OF OMAR KHAYYÁM
## The Fifth Edition, 1889

1

*WAKE! For the Sun, who scatter'd into flight*

*The Stars before him from the Field of Night,*

  *Drives Night along with them from Heav'n, and strikes*

*The Sultán's Turret with a Shaft of Light.*

2

*Before the phantom of False morning died,*

*Methought a Voice within the Tavern cried,*

  *"When all the Temple is prepared within,*

*Why nods the drowsy Worshipper outside?"*

3

*And, as the Cock crew, those who stood before*

*The Tavern shouted — "Open then the Door!*

*You know how little while we have to stay,*

*And, once departed, may return no more."*

4

*Now the New Year reviving old Desires,*

*The thoughtful Soul to Solitude retires,*

*Where the W*HITE *H*AND OF *M*OSES *on the Bough*

*Puts out, and Jesus from the Ground suspires.*

5

Iram indeed is gone with all his Rose,

And Jamshýd's Sev'n-ring'd Cup where no one knows;

But still a Ruby kindles in the Vine,

And many a Garden by the Water blows.

6

And David's Lips are lockt; but in divine

High-piping Pehleví, with "Wine! Wine! Wine!

Red Wine!" – the Nightingale cries to the Rose

That sallow cheek of hers to' incarnadine.

7

Come, fill the Cup, and in the fire of Spring

Your Winter-garment of Repentance fling:

The Bird of Time has but a little way

To flutter – and the Bird is on the Wing.

8

Whether at Naishápúr or Babylon,

Whether the Cup with sweet or bitter run,

The Wine of Life keeps oozing drop by drop,

The Leaves of Life keep falling one by one.

9

*Each Morn a thousand Roses brings, you say;*

*Yes, but where leaves the Rose of Yesterday?*

   *And this first Summer month that brings the Rose*

*Shall take Jamshýd and Kaikobád away.*

10

*Well, let it take them! What have we to do*

*With Kaikobád the Great, or Kaikhosrú?*

   *Let Zál and Rustum bluster as they will,*

*Or Hátim call to Supper — heed not you.*

11

*With me along the strip of Herbage strown*

*That just divides the desert from the sown,*

*Where name of Slave and Sultán is forgot —*

*And Peace to Mahmud on his golden Throne!*

12

*A Book of Verses underneath the Bough,*

*A Jug of Wine, a Loaf of Bread — and Thou*

*Beside me singing in the Wilderness —*

*Oh, Wilderness were Paradise enow!*

13

Some for the Glories of This World; and some

Sigh for the Prophet's Paradise to come;

  Ah, take the Cash, and let the Credit go,

Nor heed the rumble of a distant Drum!

14

Look to the blowing Rose about us — "Lo,

"Laughing," she says, "into the world I blow,

  At once the silken tassel of my Purse

Tear, and its Treasure on the Garden throw."

15

And those who husbanded the Golden grain,

And those who flung it to the winds like Rain,

Alike to no such aureate Earth are turn'd

As, buried once, Men want dug up again.

16

The Worldly Hope men set their Hearts upon

Turns Ashes – or it prospers; and anon,

Like Snow upon the Desert's dusty Face,

Lighting a little hour or two – is gone.

17

*Think, in this batter'd Caravanserai,*

*Whose Portals are alternate Night and Day,*

*How Sultán after Sultán with his Pomp*

*Abode his destined Hour, and went his way.*

18

*They say the Lion and the Lizard keep*

*The Courts where Jamshýd gloried and drank deep:*

*And Bahrám, that great Hunter — the Wild Ass*

*Stamps o'er his Head, but cannot break his Sleep.*

19

I sometimes think that never blows so red

The Rose as where some buried Cæsar bled;

That every Hyacinth the Garden wears

Dropt in her Lap from some once lovely Head.

20

And this reviving Herb whose tender Green

Fledges the River-Lip on which we lean —

Ah, lean upon it lightly! for who knows

From what once lovely Lip it springs unseen!

21

*Ah, my Belovéd, fill the Cup that clears*

*T*O-DAY *of past Regrets and future Fears:*

*To-morrow! – Why, To-morrow I may be*

*Myself with Yesterday's Sev'n thousand Years.*

22

*For some we loved, the loveliest and the best*

*That from his Vintage rolling Time hath prest,*

*Have drunk their Cup a Round or two before,*

*And one by one crept silently to rest.*

O.K.                                                     L

23

And we, that now make merry in the Room

They left, and Summer dresses in new bloom,

  Ourselves must we beneath the Couch of Earth

Descend — ourselves to make a Couch — for whom?

24

Ah, make the most of what we yet may spend,

Before we too into the Dust descend;

  Dust into Dust, and under Dust to lie,

Sans Wine, sans Song, sans Singer, and — sans Enc

25

*Alike for those who for To-DAY prepare,*

*And those that after some To-MORROW stare,*

*A Muezzin from the Tower of Darkness cries,*

*"Fools! your Reward is neither Here nor There."*

26

*Why, all the Saints and Sages who discuss'd*

*Of the Two Worlds so wisely — they are thrust*

*Like foolish Prophets forth; their Words to Scorn*

*Are scatter'd, and their Mouths are stopt with Dust.*

27

*Myself when young did eagerly frequent*

*Doctor and Saint, and heard great argument*

*About it and about: but evermore*

*Came out by the same door where in I went.*

28

*With them the seed of Wisdom did I sow,*

*And with mine own hand wrought to make it grow:*

*And this was all the Harvest that I reap'd—*

*"I came like Water, and like Wind I go."*

29

*Into this Universe, and Why not knowing*

*Nor Whence, like Water willy-nilly flowing;*

*And out of it, as Wind along the Waste,*

*I know not Whither, willy-nilly blowing.*

30

*What, without asking, hither hurried Whence?*

*And, without asking, Whither hurried hence!*

*Oh, many a Cup of this forbidden Wine*

*Must drown the memory of that insolence!*

31

Up from Earth's Centre through the Seventh Gate

I rose, and on the Throne of Saturn sate,

  And many a Knot unravel'd by the Road;

But not the Master-knot of Human Fate.

32

There was the Door to which I found no Key;

There was the Veil through which I might not see:

  Some little talk awhile of ME and THEE

There was — and then no more of THEE and ME.

33

*Earth could not answer; nor the Seas that mourn*

*In flowing Purple, of their Lord forlorn;*

*Nor rolling Heaven, with all his Signs reveal'd*

*And hidden by the sleeve of Night and Morn.*

34

*Then of the THEE IN ME who works behind*

*The Veil, I lifted up my hands to find*

*A lamp amid the Darkness; and I heard,*

*As from Without — "THE ME WITHIN THEE BLIND!"*

35

*Then to the Lip of this poor earthen Urn*

*I lean'd, the Secret of my Life to learn:*

*And Lip to Lip it murmur'd — "While you live,*

*Drink! — for, once dead, you never shall return."*

36

*I think the Vessel, that the fugitive*

*Articulation answer'd, once did live,*

*And drink; and Ah! the passive Lip I kiss'd,*

*How many Kisses might it take and give!*

37

*For I remember stopping by the way*

*To watch a Potter thumping his wet Clay:*

*And with its all-obliterated Tongue*

*It murmur'd — "Gently, Brother, gently, pray!"*

38

*And has not such a Story from of Old*

*Down Man's successive generations roll'd*

*Of such a clod of saturated Earth*

*Cast by the Maker into Human mould?*

### 39

*And not a drop that from our Cups we throw*

*For Earth to drink of, but may steal below*

*To quench the fire of Anguish in some Eye*

*There hidden — far beneath, and long ago.*

### 40

*As then the Tulip for her morning sup*

*Of Heav'nly Vintage from the soil looks up,*

*Do you devoutly do the like, till Heav'n*

*To Earth invert you — like an empty Cup.*

### 41

*Perplext no more with Human or Divine,*

*To-morrow's tangle to the winds resign,*

*And lose your fingers in the tresses of*

*The Cypress-slender Minister of Wine.*

### 42

*And if the Wine you drink, the Lip you press,*

*End in what All begins and ends in — Yes;*

*Think then you are To-day what Yesterday*

*You were — To-morrow you shall not be less.*

43

So when that Angel of the darker Drink

At last shall find you by the river-brink,

  And, offering his Cup, invite your Soul

Forth to your Lips to quaff – you shall not shrink.

44

Why, if the Soul can fling the Dust aside,

And naked on the Air of Heaven ride,

  Were't not a Shame – were't not a Shame for him

In this clay carcase crippled to abide?

### 45

*'Tis but a Tent where takes his one day's rest*

*A Sultán to the realm of Death addrest;*

*The Sultán rises, and the dark Ferrásh*

*Strikes, and prepares it for another Guest.*

### 46

*And fear not lest Existence closing your*

*Account, and mine, should know the like no more;*

*The Eternal Sákí from that Bowl has pour'd*

*Millions of Bubbles like us, and will pour.*

47

*When you and I behind the Veil are past,*

*Oh, but the long, long while the World shall last,*

*Which of our Coming and Departure heeds*

*As the Sea's self should heed a pebble-cast.*

48

*A Moment's Halt — a momentary taste*

*Of BEING from the Well amid the Waste —*

*And Lo! — the phantom Caravan has reach'd*

*The NOTHING it set out from — Oh, make haste!*

49

*Would you that spangle of Existence spend*

*About* THE SECRET — *quick about it, Friend!*

*A Hair perhaps divides the False and True —*

*And upon what, prithee, may life depend?*

50

*A Hair perhaps divides the False and True;*

*Yes; and a single Alif were the clue —*

*Could you but find it — to the Treasure-house,*

*And peradventure to* THE MASTER *too;*

51

*Whose secret Presence, through Creation's veins*

*Running Quicksilver-like eludes your pains;*

*Taking all shapes from Máh to Máhi; and*

*They change and perish all — but He remains;*

52

*A moment guess'd — then back behind the Fold*

*Immerst of Darkness round the Drama roll'd*

*Which, for the Pastime of Eternity,*

*He doth Himself contrive, enact, behold.*

5/34

## 53

*But if in vain, down on the stubborn floor*

*Of Earth, and up to Heav'n's unopening Door,*

*You gaze To-DAY, while You are You — how then*

*To-MORROW, You when shall be You no more?*

## 54

*Waste not your Hour, nor in the vain pursuit*

*Of This and That endeavour and dispute;*

*Better be jocund with the fruitful Grape*

*Than sadden after none, or bitter, Fruit.*
O.K.

55

You know, my Friends, with what a brave Carouse

I made a Second Marriage in my house;

  Divorced old barren Reason from my Bed,

And took the Daughter of the Vine to Spouse.

56

For "Is" and "Is-NOT" though with Rule and Line

And "UP-AND-DOWN" by Logic I define,

  Of all that one should care to fathom, I

Was never deep in anything but — Wine.

57

*Ah, but my Computations, People say,*

*Reduced the Year to better reckoning? — Nay,*

*'Twas only striking from the Calendar*

*Unborn To-morrow, and dead Yesterday.*

58

*And lately, by the Tavern Door agape,*

*Came shining through the Dusk an Angel Shape*

*Bearing a Vessel on his Shoulder; and*

*He bid me taste of it; and 'twas — the Grape!*

59

*The Grape that can with Logic absolute*

*The Two-and-Seventy jarring Sects confute:*

*The sovereign Alchemist that in a trice*

*Life's leaden metal into Gold transmute:*

60

*The mighty Mahmud, Allah-breathing Lord,*

*That all the misbelieving and black Horde*

*Of Fears and Sorrows that infest the Soul*

*Scatters before him with his whirlwind Sword.*

## 61

*Why, be this Juice the growth of God, who dare*

*Blaspheme the twisted tendril as a Snare?*

*A Blessing, we should use it, should we not?*

*And if a Curse — why, then, Who set it there?*

## 62

*I must abjure the Balm of Life, I must,*

*Scared by some After-reckoning ta'en on trust,*

*Or lured with Hope of some Diviner Drink,*

*To fill the Cup — when crumbled into dust!*

## 63

*Oh threats of Hell and Hopes of Paradise!*

*One thing at least is certain – This life flies;*

*One thing is certain and the rest is Lies;*

*The Flower that once has blown for ever dies.*

## 64

*Strange, is it not? that of the myriads who*

*Before us pass'd the door of Darkness through,*

*Not one returns to tell us of the Road,*

*Which to discover we must travel too.*

65

The Revelations of Devout and Learn'd

Who rose before us, and as Prophets burn'd,

  Are all but Stories, which, awoke from Sleep

They told their comrades, and to Sleep return'd.

66

I sent my Soul through the Invisible,

Some Letter of that After-life to spell:

  And by and by my Soul return'd to me,

And answer'd "I Myself am Heav'n and Hell:"

67

*Heav'n but the Vision of fulfill'd Desire,*

*And Hell the Shadow from a Soul on fire,*

*Cast on the Darkness into which Ourselves,*

*So late emerged from, shall so soon expire.*

68

*We are no other than a moving row*

*Of Magic Shadow-shapes that come and go*

*Round with the Sun-illumined Lantern held*

*In Midnight by the Master of the Show;*

69

*But helpless Pieces of the Game He plays*

*Upon this Chequer-board of Nights and Days;*

*Hither and thither moves, and checks, and slays,*

*And one by one back in the Closet lays.*

70

*The Ball no question makes of Ayes and Noes,*

*But Here or There as strikes the Player goes;*

*And He that toss'd you down into the Field,*

*He knows about it all — HE knows — HE knows!*

71

*The Moving Finger writes; and, having writ,*

*Moves on: nor all your Piety nor Wit*

  *Shall lure it back to cancel half a Line,*

*Nor all your Tears wash out a Word of it.*

72

*And that inverted Bowl they call the Sky,*

*Whereunder crawling coop'd we live and die,*

  *Lift not your hands to It for help — for It*

*As impotently moves as you or I.*

### 73

*With Earth's first Clay They did the Last Ma*

*And there of the Last Harvest sow'd the Seed:*

*And the first Morning of Creation wrote*

*What the Last Dawn of Reckoning shall read.*

74

### 74

*Y*ESTERDAY This *Day's Madness did prepare;*

*T*O-MORROW'S *Silence, Triumph, or Despair:*

*Drink! for you know not whence you came, nor why:*

*Drink! for you know not why you go, nor where.*

75

*I tell you this — When, started from the Goal,*

*Over the flaming shoulders of the Foal*

*Of Heav'n Parwín and Mushtari they flung,*

*In my predestined Plot of Dust and Soul*

76

*The Vine has struck a fibre: which about*

*If clings my Being — let the Dervish flout;*

*Of my Base metal may be filed a Key,*

*That shall unlock the Door he howls without.*

77

*And this I know: whether the one True Light*

*Kindle to Love, or Wrath-consume me quite,*

  *One Flash of It within the Tavern caught*

*Better than in the Temple lost outright.*

78

*What! out of senseless Nothing to provoke*

*A conscious Something to resent the yoke*

  *Of unpermitted Pleasure, under pain*

*Of Everlasting Penalties, if broke!*

## 79

*What! from his helpless Creature be repaid*

*Pure Gold for what he lent him dross-allay'd —*

   *Sue for a Debt he never did contract,*

*And cannot answer — Oh the sorry trade!*

## 80

*Oh Thou, who didst with pitfall and with gin*

*Beset the Road I was to wander in,*

   *Thou wilt not with Predestined Evil round*

*Enmesh, and then impute my Fall to Sin!*

81

*Oh Thou, who Man of baser Earth didst make,*

*And ev'n with Paradise devise the Snake:*

*For all the Sin wherewith the Face of Man*

*Is blacken'd — Man's forgiveness give — and take!*

82

*As under cover of departing Day*

*Slunk hunger-stricken Ramazán away,*

*Once more within the Potter's house alone*

*I stood, surrounded by the Shapes of Clay.*

83

*Shapes of all Sorts and Sizes, great and small,*

*That stood along the floor and by the wall;*

*  And some loquacious Vessels were; and some*

*Listen'd perhaps, but never talk'd at all.*

84

*Said one among them — "Surely not in vain*

*My substance of the common Earth was ta'en*

*  And to this Figure moulded, to be broke,*

*Or trampled back to shapeless Earth again."*

5/70

85

*Then said a Second — "Ne'er a peevish Boy*

*Would break the Bowl from which he drank in joy;*

*And he that with his hand the Vessel make*

*Will surely not in after Wrath destroy."*

86

*After a momentary silence spake*

*Some Vessel of a more ungainly Make;*

*"They sneer at me for leaning all awry:*

*What! did the Hand then of the Potter shake?"*

87

*Whereat some one of the loquacious Lot —*

*I think a Sufi pipkin — waxing hot —*

　*"All this of Pot and Potter — Tell me, then,*

*Who is the Potter, pray, and who the Pot?"*

88

*"Why," said another, "Some there are who tell*

*Of one who threatens he will toss to Hell*

　*The luckless Pots he marr'd in making — Pish!*

*He's a Good Fellow, and 'twill all be well."*

89

*"Well," murmur'd one, "Let whoso make or buy,*

*My Clay with long Oblivion is gone dry:*

*But fill me with the old familiar Juice,*

*Methinks I might recover by and by."*

90

*So while the Vessels one by one were speaking,*

*The little Moon look'd in that all were seeking:*

*And then they jogg'd each other, "Brother! Brother!*

*Now for the Porter's shoulder-knot a-creaking!"*

91

*Ah, with the Grape my fading life provide,*

*And wash the Body whence the Life has died,*

*And lay me, shrouded in the living Leaf,*

*By some not unfrequented Garden-side.*

92

*That ev'n my buried Ashes such a snare*

*Of Vintage shall fling up into the Air*

*As not a True-believer passing by*

*But shall be overtaken unaware.*

93

*Indeed the Idols I have loved so long*

*Have done my credit in this World much wrong:*

*Have drown'd my Glory in a shallow Cup,*

*And sold my Reputation for a Song.*

94

*Indeed, Indeed, Repentance oft before*

*I swore – but was I sober when I swore?*

*And then and then came Spring, and Rose-in-hand*

*My thread-bare Penitence apieces tore.*

## 95

And much as Wine has play'd the Infidel,

And robb'd me of my Robe of Honour – Well,

   I wonder often what the Vintners buy

One half so precious as the stuff they sell.

## 96

Yet Ah, that Spring should vanish with the Rose!

That Youth's sweet-scented manuscript should close!

   The Nightingale that in the branches sang,

Ah whence, and whither flown again, who knows!

97

*Would but the Desert of the Fountain yield*

*One glimpse — if dimly, yet indeed, reveal'd,*

*To which the fainting Traveller might spring,*

*As springs the trampled herbage of the field!*

98

*Would but some wingéd Angel ere too late*

*Arrest the yet unfolded Roll of Fate,*

*And make the stern Recorder otherwise*

*Enregister, or quite obliterate!*

99

*Ah Love! could you and I with Him conspire*

*To grasp this sorry Scheme of Things entire,*

*Would not we shatter it to bits — and then*

*Re-mould it nearer to the Heart's Desire!*

100

*Yon rising Moon that looks for us again —*

*How oft hereafter will she wax and wane;*

*How oft hereafter rising look for us*

*Through this same Garden — and for one in vain!*

## IOI

*And when like her, oh Sákí, you shall pass*

*Among the Guests Star-scatter'd on the Grass,*

*And in your joyous errand reach the spot*

*Where I made One – turn down an empty Glass!*

## TAMÁM

# NOTE BY W. ALDIS WRIGHT

*(Added to the Fifth Edition)*

It must be admitted that FitzGerald took great liberties with the original in his version of Omar Khayyám. The first stanza is entirely his own, in stanza 33 of the fourth edition (36 in the second) he has introduced two lines from Attár (see Letters 1,320). In stanza 81 (fourth edition), writes Professor Cowell, "There is no original for the line about the snake: I have looked for it in vain in Nicholas; but I have always supposed that the last line is FitzGerald's mistaken version of Quatr. 236 in Nicholas's ed. which runs thus:

> O thou who knowest the secrets of every one's mind,
> Who graspest every one's hand in the hour of weakness,
> O God, give me repentance and accept my excuses,
> O thou who givest repentance and acceptest the excuses of every one.

FitzGerald mistook the meaning of *giving* and *accepting* as used here, and so invented his last line out of his own mistake. I wrote to him about it when I was in Calcutta; but he never cared to alter it."

# VARIATIONS IN TEXTS

*First Edition* (1859)

Quatrain 45 was not included in subsequent editions.

*Second Edition* (1868)

Quatrains 14, 28, 44, 65, 77, 86, 99 and 107 were not included in subsequent editions. Quatrain 20 was not included in the text in later editions but was quoted in the *note* to Quatrain 18 in the Third and Fourth Editions.

*Third Edition* (1872)

Quatrain 10, lines 3 and 4 read:
> *Let Zál and Rustum thunder as they will,*
> Or Hátim *call* to Supper – heed not you.

Quatrain 12, lines 1 and 2 read:
> *A Book of Verses underneath* the Bough,
> *A Jug of Wine, a Loaf of Bread* – and Thou

Quatrain 13, lines 3 and 4 read:
> Ah, take the Cash, and let the *Credit* go,
> Nor heed the *rumble* of a distant Drum!

Quatrain 20 (25 in the 2nd Ed.) lines 1 and 2 read:
> And this *reviving* Herb whose *tender* Green
> Fledges the *River*-Lip on which we lean –

Quatrain 21, line 2 reads:
> Today of past *Regret* and future Fears:

Quatrain 27 (30 in the 2nd Ed.) line 4 reads:
> Came out by the same door *where* in I went.

Quatrain 30 (33 in the 2nd Ed.) lines 3 and 4 read:
> *Oh, many a Cup of this forbidden Wine*
> *Must drown* the memory of that insolence!

203

Quatrain 31 (34 in the 2nd Ed.) line 3 reads:
And many *a Knot* unravel'd by the Road;

Quatrain 33 (36 in the 2nd Ed.) line 3 reads:
Nor *rolling Heaven, with all his* Signs reveal'd

Quatrain 34 (37 in the 2nd Ed.) reads:
Then of the Thee in Me who works behind
The Veil, *I lifted up my hands* to find
A Lamp *amid the Darkness; and I heard,*
*As from Without* – " *THE ME WITHIN THEE BLIND!*"

Quatrain 35 (38 in the 2nd Ed.) line 2 reads:
I lean'd, the Secret *of my* Life to learn:

Quatrain 36 (39 in the 2nd Ed.) line 3 reads:
And drink; and *Ah! the passive* Lip I kiss'd,

Quatrain 38 in the Third edition (which appears in this edition only) reads:
Listen – a moment listen! – Of the same
Poor Earth from which that Human Whisper came
The luckless Mould in which Mankind was cast
They did compose, and call'd him by the name.

Quatrain 39 (42 in the 2nd Ed.) line 2 reads:
*For Earth to drink of,* but may steal below

Quatrain 40 (43 in the 2nd Ed.) lines 1, 2 and 3 read:
As then the Tulip for her *morning* sup
Of Heav'nly Vintage *from the soil looks* up,
Do you *devoutly do the like,* till Heav'n

Quatrain 41 (55 in the 2nd Ed.) lines 1 and 2 read:
*Perplext* no more with Human or Divine,
To-morrow's tangle to *the winds* resign,

Quatrain 42 (45 in the 2nd Ed.) reads:
And if the *Wine* you drink, the Lip you press,
End in what All begins and ends in – Yes;
*Think* then you are *TO-DAY what YESTERDAY*
YOU were – *TO-MORROW* you shall not be less.

Quatrain 43 (46 in the 2nd Ed.) reads:
> So when *the* Angel *of the darker Drink*
> *At last shall find* you by the river-brink,
>     And, *offering* his Cup, *invite* your Soul
> Forth to your Lips to quaff – *you shall* not shrink.

Quatrain 44 (69 in the 2nd Ed.) lines 3 and 4 read:
>     *Wer't* not a Shame – *wer't* not a Shame for him
> *In this clay carcase crippled* to abide?

Quatrain 45 (70 in the 2nd Ed.) line 1 reads:
> *'Tis* but a Tent *where takes his one-day's* rest

Quatrain 46 (47 in the 2nd Ed.) line 2 reads:
> Account, *and mine, should know the like* no more;

Quatrain 47 (48 in the 2nd Ed.) line 4 reads:
> As *the Sev'n Seas should heed* a pebble-cast.

Quatrain 48 (49 in the 2nd Ed.) reads:
> *A Moment's Halt – a momentary taste*
> *Of BEING from the Well amid the Waste –*
>     *And Lo! – the phantom Caravan has reach'd*
> *The NOTHING it set out from –* Oh, make haste!

Quatrain 49 (50 in the 2nd Ed.) line 3 reads:
> A Hair *perhaps* divides the False and True –

Quatrain 50 (51 in the 2nd Ed.) line 1 reads:
> A Hair *perhaps* divides the False and True;

Quatrain 54 (56 in the 2nd Ed.) line 3 reads:
> Better be *jocund* with the fruitful Grape

Quatrain 55 (57 in the 2nd Ed.) lines 1 and 2 read:
>     You know, my Friends, *with what a brave Carouse*
> *I made a Second Marriage in my house;*

Quatrain 57 (59 in the 2nd Ed.) lines 2 and 3 read:
> *Reduced the Year to better reckoning? – Nay,*
>     *'Twas only* striking from the Calendar

Quatrain 62 (64 in the 2nd Ed.) line 4 reads:
*To fill the Cup — when* crumbled into Dust!

Quatrain 66 (71 in the 2nd Ed.) lines 3 and 4 read:
*And by and by my Soul return'd to me,*
And *answer'd* "*I* Myself am Heav'n and Hell."

Quatrain 81 (88 in the 2nd Ed.) lines 3 and 4 read:
For all the Sin *wherewith the Face of* Man
Is *blacken'd — Man's Forgiveness give —* and take!

Quatrain 84 (91 in the 2nd Ed.) lines 3 and 4 read:
"*And to this Figure moulded, to be broke,*
*Or trampled* back to shapeless Earth again."

Quatrain 85 (92 in the 2nd Ed.) reads:
*Then said a Second —* "Ne'er a peevish Boy
"Would break the *Bowl* from which he drank in joy;
"*And He that with his hand the Vessel* made
"*Will surely not in after Wrath* destroy!"

Quatrain 86 (93 in the 2nd Ed.) line 1 reads:
*After a momentary* silence spake

Quatrain 87 (94 in the 2nd Ed.) reads:
*Whereat some one of the loquacious Lot —*
*I think a Sufi pipkin — waxing hot —*
*"All this of Pot and Potter — Tell me, then,*
*"Who makes — Who sells — Who buys — Who is the Pot?"*

Quatrain 88 (95 in the 2nd Ed.) lines 1, 2 and 3 read:
*"Why," said another, "Some there are who* tell
*"Of one who threatens he will toss to* Hell
*"The luckless Pots he marr'd in making —* Pish!

Quatrain 89 (96 in the 2nd Ed.) line 1 reads:
"Well," *murmur'd one, "Let whoso make or buy,*

Quatrain 90 (97 in the 2nd Ed.) line 2 reads:
*The little Moon look'd in that* all were seeking:

Quatrain 91 (98 in the 2nd Ed.) line 2 reads:
> And wash *the* Body whence the Life has died,

Quatrain 95 (103 in the 2nd Ed.) lines 3 and 4 read:
> I *wonder often* what the Vintners buy
> One half so precious as the *stuff* they sell.

Quatrain 97 (105 in the 2nd Ed.) line 3 reads:
> *To* which the fainting Traveller might spring,

Quatrain 98 (106 in the 2nd Ed.) reads:
> *Would but some wingéd Angel ere too late*
> *Arrest the Yet unfolded Roll* of Fate,
>   And make *the stern Recorder otherwise*
> *Enregister*, or quite obliterate!

Quatrain 99 (108 in the 2nd Ed.) line 1 reads:
> Ah Love! could you and I with *Him* conspire

Quatrain 100 (109 in the 2nd Ed.) reads:
> *Yon* rising Moon *that looks for us* again –
> *How oft hereafter will she wax and wane;*
>   How oft hereafter rising *look for us*
> *Through this same Garden – an for one* in vain!

Quatrain 101 (110 in the 2nd Ed.) lines 1, 2 and 3 read:
> And when *like her, Oh Sákí, you* shall pass
> Among the Guests Star-scatter'd on the Grass,
>   And in your *blissful* errand reach the spot

*Fourth Edition* (1879)

The actual variations between the Fourth and Fifth Editions are slight and consist mainly of literals and punctuation as shown in the following table:

| *Quatrain* | *Fourth Edition* | *Fifth Edition* |
|---|---|---|
| 1, Line 1 | Sun | Sun, |
| 6, ,, 4 | her's | hers |
| 16, ,, 4 | was gone | is gone |
| 17, ,, 4 | Destin'd | destined |
| 21, ,, 2 | Regret | Regrets |
| 24, ,, 3 | under Dust, | under Dust |
| 43, ,, 1 | the Angel | that Angel |
| 44, ,, 3 | Wer't | Were't |
| 48, ,, 3 | reacht | reach'd |
| 49, ,, 4 | does | may |
| 56, ,, 1 | Line, | Line |
| 67, ,, 2 | fire | fire, |
| 67, ,, 4 | emerg'd | emerged |
| 68, ,, 3 | illumin'd | illumined |
| 74, ,, 2 | TO-MORROW'S | To-Morrow's |
| 75, ,, 4 | predestin'd | predestined |
| 79, ,, 3 | we | he |
| 80, ,, 3 | Predestin'd | Predestined |

# COMPARATIVE TABLE OF QUATRAINS
## IN THE FIVE VERSIONS

| First<br>Edition | Second<br>Edition | Third, Fourth<br>and Fifth<br>Editions |
|:---:|:---:|:---:|
| 1 | 1 | 1 |
| 2 | 2 | 2 |
| 3 | 3 | 3 |
| 4 | 4 | 4 |
| 5 | 5 | 5 |
| 6 | 6 | 6 |
| 7 | 7 | 7 |
| 8 | 9 | 9 |
| 9 | 10 | 10 |
| 10 | 11 | 11 |
| 11 | 12 | 12 |
| 12 | 13 | 13 |
| 13 | 15 | 14 |
| 14 | 17 | 16 |
| 15 | 16 | 15 |
| 16 | 18 | 17 |
| 17 | 19 | 18 |
| 18 | 24 | 19 |
| 19 | 25 | 20 |
| 20 | 21 | 21 |
| 21 | 22 | 22 |
| 22 | 23 | 23 |
| 23 | 26 | 24 |
| 24 | 27 | 25 |
| 25 | 29 | 26 |
| 26 | 66 | 63 |
| 27 | 30 | 27 |
| 28 | 31 | 28 |

| First Edition | Second Edition | Third, Fourth and Fifth Editions |
|---|---|---|
| 29 | 32 | 29 |
| 30 | 33 | 30 |
| 31 | 34 | 31 |
| 32 | 35 | 32 |
| 33 | 37 | 34 |
| 34 | 38 | 35 |
| 35 | 39 | 36 |
| 36 | 40 | 37 |
| 37 | | |
| 38 | 49 | 48 |
| 39 | 56 | 54 |
| 40 | 57 | 55 |
| 41 | 58 | 56 |
| 42 | 60 | 58 |
| 43 | 61 | 59 |
| 44 | 62 | 60 |
| 45 | | |
| 46 | 73 | 68 |
| 47 | 45 | 42 |
| 48 | 46 | 43 |
| 49 | 74 | 69 |
| 50 | 75 | 70 |
| 51 | 76 | 71 |
| 52 | 78 | 72 |
| 53 | 79 | 73 |
| 54 | 81 | 75 |
| 55 | 82 | 76 |
| 56 | 83 | 77 |
| 57 | 87 | 80 |
| 58 | 88 | 81 |
| 59 | 89 | 82 |
| 60 | 94 | 87 |

| First Edition | Second Edition | Third, Fourth and Fifth Editions |
|---|---|---|
| 61 | 91 | 84 |
| 62 | 92 | 85 |
| 63 | 93 | 86 |
| 64 | 95 | 88 |
| 65 | 96 | 89 |
| 66 | 97 | 90 |
| 67 | 98 | 91 |
| 68 | 100 | 92 |
| 69 | 101 | 93 |
| 70 | 102 | 94 |
| 71 | 103 | 95 |
| 72 | 104 | 96 |
| 73 | 108 | 99 |
| 74 | 109 | 100 |
| 75 | 110 | 101 |
|  | 8 | 8 |
|  | 14 |  |
|  | 20 |  |
|  | 28 |  |
|  | 36 | 33 |
|  | 41 | 38 |
|  | 42 | 39 |
|  | 43 | 40 |
|  | 44 |  |
|  | 47 | 46 |
|  | 48 | 47 |
|  | 50 | 49 |
|  | 51 | 50 |
|  | 52 | 51 |
|  | 53 | 52 |
|  | 54 | 53 |
|  | 55 | 41 |

| First Edition | Second Edition | Third, Fourth and Fifth Editions |
|---|---|---|
|  | 59 | 57 |
|  | 63 | 61 |
|  | 64 | 62 |
|  | 65 |  |
|  | 67 | 64 |
|  | 68 | 65 |
|  | 69 | 44 |
|  | 70 | 45 |
|  | 71 | 66 |
|  | 72 | 67 |
|  | 77 |  |
|  | 80 | 74 |
|  | 84 | 78 |
|  | 85 | 79 |
|  | 86 |  |
|  | 90 | 83 |
|  | 99 |  |
|  | 105 | 97 |
|  | 106 | 98 |
|  | 107 |  |

# NOTES TO SECOND EDITION

*The numbers refer to the Quatrains of the Second Edition.*

2    The "*False Dawn*"; *Subhi Kázib*, a transient Light on the Horizon about an hour before the *Subhi sádik*, or True Dawn; a well-known Phenomenon in the East.

4    New Year. Beginning with the Vernal Equinox, it must be remembered; and (howsoever the old Solar Year is practically superseded by the clumsy *Lunar* Year that dates from the Mohammedan Hijra) still commemorated by a Festival that is said to have been appointed by the very Jamshýd whom Omar so often talks of, and whose yearly Calendar he helped to rectify.

      "The sudden approach and rapid advance of the Spring," says Mr. Binning [*Two Years' Travel in Persia &c* 1.165] "are very striking. Before the Snow is well off the Ground, the Trees burst into Blossom, and the Flowers start forth from the Soil. At *Now Rooz* [*their* New Year's Day] the Snow was lying in patches on the Hills and in the shaded Vallies, while the Fruit-trees in the Gardens were budding beautifully, and green Plants and Flowers springing up on the Plains on every side –

> '*And on old Hyems' Chin and icy Crown*
> '*An odorous Chaplet of sweet Summer buds*
> '*Is, as in mockery, set.*' –

      Among the Plants newly appeared I recognised some old Acquaintances I had not seen for many a Year: among these, two varieties of the Thistle – a coarse species of Daisy like the 'Horse-gowan' – red and white Clover – the Dock – the blue Cornflower – and that vulgar Herb the Dandelion rearing its yellow crest on the Banks of the Water-courses." The Nightingale was not yet heard, for the Rose was not yet blown: but an almost identical Blackbird and Woodpecker helped to make up something of a North-country Spring.

4    "The White Hand of Moses." Exodus iv. 6; where Moses draws forth his Hand – not, according to the Persians, "*leprous as Snow*" – but *white*, as our May-blossom in Spring perhaps. According to them also the Healing Power of Jesus resided in his Breath.

5    Iram, planted by King Shaddád, and now sunk somewhere in the Sands of Arabia. Jamshýd's Seven-ring'd Cup was typical of the 7 Heavens, 7 Planets, 7 Seas, &c., and was a *Divining Cup*.

6  *Pehleví*, the old Heroic *Sanskrit* of Persia. Háfiz also speaks of the Nightingale's
*Pehleví*, which did not change with the People's.

6  I am not sure if the fourth line refers to the Red Rose looking sickly, or to the Yellow Rose that ought to be Red; Red, White, and Yellow Roses all common in
Persia. I think that Southey, in his Common-Place Book, quotes from some
Spanish author about the Rose being White till 10 o'clock; "Rosa Perfecta" at 2;
and "perfecta incarnada" at 5.

10  Rustum, the "Hercules" of Persia, and Zál his Father, whose exploits are among
the most celebrated in the Shah-nama. Hátim Tai, a well-known type of Oriental
Generosity.

13  A Drum – beaten outside a Palace.

15  That is, the Rose's Golden Centre.

19  Persepolis: call'd also *Takht-i-Jamshýd* – THE THRONE OF JAMSHÝD, "*King Splen-
did*," of the mythical *Peshdádian* Dynasty, and supposed (according to the Shah-
nama) to have been founded and built by him.

19  Others refer it to the Work of the Genie King, Ján Ibn Ján – who also built the
Pyramids – before the time of Adam.

19  BAHRÁM GUR – *Bahram of the Wild Ass* – a Sassanian Sovereign – had also his Seven
Castles (like the King of Bohemia!) each of a different Colour: each with a Royal
Mistress within; each of whom tells him a Story, as told in one of the most famous
Poems of Persia, written by Amir Khusraw: all these Sevens also figuring (accord-
ing to Eastern Mysticism) the Seven Heavens; and perhaps the Book itself that
Eighth, into which the mystical Seven transcend, and within which they revolve.
The Ruins of Three of those Towers are yet shown by the Peasantry; as also the
Swamp in which Bahrám sunk, like the Master of Ravenswood, while pursuing
his *Gúr*.

20
> *The Palace that to Heav'n his pillars threw,*
> *And Kings the forehead on his threshold drew –*
> *I saw the solitary Ringdove there,*
> *And "Coo, coo, coo," she cried; and "Coo, coo, coo."*

This Quatrain Mr. Binning found, among several of Háfiz and others, inscribed
by some stray hand among the ruins of Persepolis. The Ringdove's ancient *Pehleví*

*Coo, Coo, Coo,* signifies also in Persian *"Where? Where? Where?"* In Attár's "Bird-parliament" she is reproved by the Leader of the Birds for sitting still, and for ever harping on that one note of lamentation for her lost Yúsuf.

21   A thousand years to each Planet.

24   Apropos of Omar's Red Roses in Stanza 24, I am reminded of an old English Superstition, that our Anemone Pulsatilla, or purple "Pasque Flower" (which grows plentifully about the Fleam Dyke, near Cambridge), grows only where Danish Blood has been spilt.

34   Saturn, Lord of the Seventh Heaven.

35   ME-AND-THEE: some dividual Existence or Personality distinct from the Whole.

40   One of the Persian Poets – Attár, I think – has a pretty story about this. A thirsty Traveller dips his hand into a Spring of Water to drink from. By-and-by comes another who draws up and drinks from an earthen Bowl, and then departs, leaving his Bowl behind him. The first Traveller takes it up for another draught; but is surprised to find that the same Water which had tasted sweet from his own hand tastes bitter from the earthen Bowl. But a Voice – from Heaven, I think – tells him the clay from which the Bowl is made was once *Man*; and, into whatever shape renewed, can never lose the bitter flavour of Mortality.

42   The custom of throwing a little Wine on the ground before drinking still continues in Persia, and perhaps generally in the East. Mons. Nicolas considers it "un signe de libéralité, et en même temps un avertissement que le buveur doit vider sa coupe jusqu'à la dernière goutte." Is it not more likely an ancient Superstition; a Libation to propitiate Earth, or make her an Accomplice in the illicit Revel? Or, perhaps, to divert the Jealous Eye by some sacrifice of superfluity, as with the Ancients of the West? With Omar we see something more is signified; the precious Liquor is not lost, but sinks into the ground to refresh the dust of some poor Wine-worshipper foregone.

   Thus Háfiz, copying Omar in so many ways: "When thou drinkest Wine pour a draught on the ground. Wherefore fear the Sin which brings to another Gain?"

46   According to one beautiful Oriental Legend, Azräel accomplishes his mission by holding to the nostril an Apple from the Tree of Life.

   This and the two following Stanzas would have been withdrawn, as some what *de trop*, from the Text, but for advice which I least like to disregard.

52    From Máh to Máhi: from Fish to Moon.

58    A Jest, of course, at his Studies. A curious mathematical Quatrain of Omar's has been pointed out to me; the more curious because almost exactly parallel'd by some Verses of Doctor Donne's, that are quoted in Izaak Walton's Lives! Here is Omar: "You and I are the image of a pair of compasses; though we have two heads (sc. our *feet*) we have one body; when we have fixed the centre for our circle, we bring our heads (sc. feet) together at the end." Dr. Donne:

> *If we be two, we two are so*
> *As stiff twin-compasses are two;*
> *Thy Soul, the fixt foot, makes no show*
> *To move, but does if the other do.*
>
> *And though thine in the centre sit,*
> *Yet when my other far does roam,*
> *Thine leans and hearkens after it,*
> *And grows erect as mine comes home.*
>
> *Such thou must be to me, who must*
> *Like the other foot obliquely run;*
> *Thy firmness makes my circle just,*
> *And me to end where I begun.*

61    The Seventy-two Religions supposed to divide the World, *including* Islamism, as some think: but others not.

62    Alluding to Sultán Mahmud's Conquest of India and its dark people.

73    *Fanusi khiyal*, a Magic-lantern still used in India; the cylindrical Interior being painted with various Figures, and so lightly poised and ventilated as to revolve round the lighted Candle within.

75    A very mysterious Line in the Original
          *O danad O danad O danad O –*
     breaking off something like our Woodpigeon's Note, which she is said to take up just where she left off.

81    Parwín and Mushtari – The Pleiads and Jupiter.

94 This Relation of Pot and Potter to Man and his Maker figures far and wide in the Literature of the World, from the time of the Hebrew Prophets to the present; when it may finally take the name of "Pot theism," by which Mr. Carlyle ridiculed Sterling's "Pantheism." *My* Sheikh, whose knowledge flows in from all quarters, writes to me:

"Apropos of old Omar's Pots, did I ever tell you the sentence I found in 'Bishop Pearson on the Creed'? 'Thus are we wholly at the disposal of His will, and our present and future condition framed and ordered by His free, but wise and just, decrees. *Hath not the potter power over the clay, of the same lump to make one vessel unto honour, and another unto dishonour*? (Rom. ix 21). And can that earth-artificer have a freer power over his *brother potsherd* (both being made of the same metal), than God hath over him, who, by the strange fecundity of His omnipotent power, first made the clay out of nothing, and then him out of that?' " And again – from a very different quarter – "I had to refer the other day to Aristophanes, and came by chance on a curious Speaking-pot story in the Vespae (*The Wasps*, lines 1435-40), which I had quite forgotten.

"The Pot calls a bystander to be a witness to his bad treatment. The woman says, 'If, by Proserpine, instead of all this "testifying" (comp. Cuddie and his mother in "Old Mortality!") you would buy yourself a rivet, it would show more sense in you!' The Scholiast explains *echinus* as any bowl from the potter."

One more illustration for the oddity's sake from the "Autobiography of a Cornish Rector," by the late James Hamley Tregenna, 1871.

"There was one old Fellow in our Company – he was so like a Figure in the 'Pilgrim's Progress' that Richard always called him the 'ALLEGORY' with a long white beard – a rare Appendage in those days – and a Face the colour of which seemed to have been baked in, like the Faces one used to see on Earthenware Jugs. In our Country-dialect Earthenware is called '*Clome*'; so the Boys of the Village used to shout out after him – 'Go back to the Potter, old Clome-face, and get baked over again.' For the 'Allegory,' though shrewd enough in most things, had the reputation of being '*saift-baked*,' i.e., of weak intellect."

97 At the Close of the Fasting Month, Ramazán (which makes the Musulman unhealthy and unamiable), the first Glimpse of the New Moon (who rules their division of the Year), is looked for with the utmost Anxiety, and hailed with Acclamation. Then it is that the Porter's Knot may be heard – toward the *Cellar*. Omar has elsewhere a pretty Quatrain about the same Moon:

> "*Be of Good Cheer – the sullen Month will die,*
> *And a young Moon requite us by and by:*
> *Look how the Old one meagre, bent, and wan*
> *With Age and Fast, is fainting from the Sky!*"

# GLOSSARY

ALIF [*a'-lif*]  The first letter in the Persian alphabet.

ALLAH [*al'-lā*]  Arabic name for God. The Absolute.

AMIR [*a-meer'*]  Prince.

ASSÁR [*as'-sār*]  Oil pressers.

ATTÁR [*at'-tār*]  Druggist.

ATTÁR  The Persian poet Farrîd-uddîn Attâr, author of *The Mantik-ut-Tair,* i.e., Parliament of the Birds.

BAHRÁM GUR [*bah'-rām goor*]  Bahram of the Wild Ass, Persian king and hunter.

CARAVANSERAI [*kar-a-van'-se-ray*]  Inn where caravans rest at night.

DANAD  He knows, third person singular of *dân,* to know.

FANUSI KHIYAL [*fā-noo'-see khee'-yal*]  Magic lantern.

FERRÁSH [*fer-rāsh*]  Servant, tent-pitcher.

HÁFIZ [*hā-fiz*]  Persian lyric poet (d. 1389).

HÁTIM TAI [*hā'-tim tye*]  A pre-Islamic Arab famed for his generosity.

HIJRA, more commonly HEGIRA [*he-jye-ra*]  The migration of Muhammad from Mecca to Medina in A.D. 622 from which Muslims date their era.

IMÁM [*i-mām'*]  A Muhammadan leader of prayer.

IRAM [*ee'-ram*]  A fabulous garden supposed to have been planted in Arabia by Shaddád bin Ad.

JÁMI [*jā'-mi*]  Persian poet (d. 1492).

JAMSHÝD [*Jam'-sheed*]  Mythical Persian king. According to Firdausî he reigned seven hundred years. His palace was at Persepolis.

JELÁLUDDIN [*je-lāl'-ud-deen*]  Malikshah. A Saljuk sultán (1072-1092).

KAIKHOSRÚ [*Kye'-khos-roo*]  Mythical Persian king.

KAIKOBÁD [*kye'-ko-bād*]  Mythical king.

KHORÁSÁN [*kho-rā-sān'*]  The largest of the Persian provinces where Omar was born.

KUZA-NAMA [*koo'-za nā'-ma*]  Book of pots, title given to stanzas 59-66 in first edition of the *Rubáiyát.*

MÁH  Moon.

MÁHI  Fish.

MAHMUD [*mah'-mood*]  King of Ghazna, b. 969, d. 1030.

MIHRÁB [*mee-rāb*]  The niche in a mosque which indicates the direction of Mecca towards which the Muslim worshipper turns in prayer.

MUEZZIN [*moo-ez'-zin*]  Muhammadan crier of the hour of prayer.

MUSHTARI [*mush'-ta-ree*]  The planet Jupiter.

NAISHÁPÚR [*nay'-shā-poor*]  Nishapur, the city of Khorásán, Iran, where Omar was born.

# GLOSSARY

Now Rooz  New Year's Day.

Nizám ul Mulk [*nee-zām' ool moolk'*]  Vizier to Alp Arslan the Younger.

Omar Khayyám [*o'mar khye-yahm'*]  Persian philosopher, astronomer and poet, author of *The Rubáiyát,* who died in 1132.

Parwín [*par'-ween*]  The constellation of the Pleiades.

Pehleví [*peh'-le-vee*]  The principal language of the Persians from the third to the ninth centuries A.D.

Ramazán [*ram-a-zān*]  Ramadan, the ninth month of the Muhammadan year, devoted to strict fasting.

Rubáiyát [*roo'-bye-yāt*]  Plural of the Arabic word *rubáiyáh,* a quatrain or stanza of four lines.

Rustum [*rus'-tum*]  A mythical Persian hero, son of Zál and father of Sohráb in the *Shah-nama.*

Sákí [*sā-kee*]  Cupbearer.

Shah-Nama  *The Book of Kings* by Abul Kasim Mansur, better known as Firdausî.

Sheikh [*shaykh*]  An Arabian chief; literally, old man.

Subhi Kazib [*soob'-hee kā'-zib*]  False dawn.

Subhi Sadik [*soob'-hee sā'-dik*]  True dawn.

Sufi [*sŏo'-fee*]  Muhammadan mystic. The elaborate Sufi symbolism was much used by the poets.

Sultán [*sul-tān*]  King.

Takhallus [*ta-khal-lus*]  Pen-name used by Persian poets; for example, Abul Kasim Mansur, author of the *Shah-nama,* called himself Firdausî from Firdaus which means *Paradise.* Omar called himself Khayyám, i.e., Tent-maker.

Tamám [*ta-mām*]  The end.

Tamám Shud [*ta-mām' shood*]  The very end.

Vizier [*vi-zeer'*]  A minister or counsellor of state.

Zál [*zāl*]  The father of Rustum.

# INDEX TO FIRST LINES OF QUATRAINS

# INDEX TO FIRST LINES OF QUATRAINS

# INDEX TO FIRST LINES OF QUATRAINS

# INDEX TO FIRST LINES OF QUATRAINS

# INDEX TO FIRST LINES OF QUATRAINS